AN ACTIVE RETIREMENT

Nancy Tuft

BOOKS

© 1992 Nancy Tuft
Published by Age Concern England
1268 London Road
London SW16 4ER

Editor   Claire Llewellyn
Design   Eugenie Dodd
Production   Marion Peat
Printed and bound in Great Britain by
Bell & Bain Ltd, Glasgow

A catalogue record for this book is available
from the British Library.

ISBN 0–86242–119–5

Contents

Sponsor's foreword

Dear reader

Welcome to *An Active Retirement*. Stannah Stairlifts is delighted to support this important publication which provides essential advice to a growing sector of the population.

Many of us look forward to retirement, when we can finally find the time to pursue all those activities which we never seem to have enough time for, such as travelling, gardening, listening to music, reading, playing bridge or learning another language. The options are endless . . .

For some of us, however, the idea of having extra time on our hands can be daunting. Ageing is something which happens to us all, and confidence plays a crucial role in leading an active, fulfilled life at any age.

This practical guide is bursting with information on hobbies, sports, educational opportunities and voluntary work and is ideal for retired people seeking new ways to fill their time but who are uncertain where to start.

Stannah Stairlifts is renowned for taking the strain out of climbing stairs, so you can both stay on in the home and neighbourhood you love and devote your energies to more pleasurable activities such as exercise or your favourite hobbies.

This is why we are delighted to be associated with Age Concern in producing *An Active Retirement* and we are confident that you will find this guide a stimulating and enjoyable kaleidoscope of activity ideas.

Wishing you all a very happy and active retirement.

Yours

David Walton
Managing Director
Stannah Stairlifts

About the author

Nancy Tuft is an experienced author and journalist who specialises in writing for and about older people. Previous titles published by Age Concern include *Life in the Sun*, a guide to long-stay holidays and living abroad in retirement, and *Looking Good, Feeling Good*, a challenging and positive look at the importance of style and personal appearance in later life.

She has tutored a series of retirement courses for Bromley Adult Education Service, as well as leading lifestyle sessions in seminars on retirement guidance.

Aged 59, with three adult children and five grandchildren, Nancy Tuft lives in Bromley where she is an active member of the local University of the Third Age.

Acknowledgements

Retirement is about growing up as well as about coming to terms with growing old. No two people face the future in quite the same way and I am grateful to the many and varied retired people who have shared their experiences, both good and not so good, with me over the years.

In spite of the active involvement in retirement courses and seminars, it wasn't until my own partner's retirement that the awful truth dawned on me. You can't live someone else's life for them. People really do have to find their own way, and in their own time. Hopefully this book may be of use.

I appreciate the ideas and suggestions put forward by both Liz Dendy, recently retired from the Sports Council, and Dianne Norton, Education and Leisure Officer at Age Concern England. Also at Age Concern my thanks go to Evelyn McEwen, David Moncrieff, Gill Cronin and Lee Bennett for their on-going interest and valuable input. Thank you too to editor Claire Llewellyn for her customary clear-sightedness.

Nancy Tuft
October 1992

CHAPTER ONE

A change of lifestyle

All things must change to something new, to something strange.

HENRY WADSWORTH LONGFELLOW

When you work full-time, leisure is merely the leftovers, whatever you can manage to cram into life's few remaining hours. By the time you've shopped, mowed the lawn, cleaned the house, cooked, done the occasional DIY or decorating job, visited relatives and dealt with the hundred and one little extras, there is precious little time left. There is never enough time for yourself.

Now you're retired, things are going to be different. It's time for a reappraisal of leisure. A week consists of 168 hours. Approximately 50–60 hours are spent sleeping. Another 50–60 hours are taken up with routine maintenance of both our homes and ourselves. This leaves the 50 or so hours which used to be consumed by work. They are now all yours. If you can get it right, these should be 50 full and shining hours – quality time. This wonderful new existence will not materialise overnight, however. It will require considerable input from you; a serious re-think, followed by some reorganisation of your existing way of life. Time management begins to take on a new meaning.

The words 'a change of lifestyle' imply a way of living which is *chosen*, not inflicted. Gone is the idea of 'the daily round'. What lifestyle do you seek for your retirement?

Retirement today: the third age

People retiring in the 1990s can expect to spend nearly as long in retirement as they did at work. It can amount to one-third of your lifetime. The word 'retirement' is really an anachronism, and nowadays 'the third age' is a term which is increasingly used. It refers to the mentally fit and active years after paid work, a period which for many people may last for the rest of their lives. The first age consists of childhood and growing up; the second age covers the adult work and parenting phase; the fourth age, where it applies, may be a very short period of frailty and dependence. Many people skip this stage altogether. For others it may last only a few months.

The importance of the third age is that it is yours to enjoy. It is as valid and significant as the period of paid employment. In fact, it is in this period of life that many people discover talents and skills they never knew they possessed. Assuming an adequate income, the new circumstances of the third age demand a reassessment of priorities. How do you feel about your retirement?

Responses to retirement

A retirement guidance consultant has defined three broad categories of retirement responses:

Can't wait

Why me?

Whatever shall I do?

CAN'T WAIT

This group includes people whose jobs have become increasingly stressful and unsatisfying for whatever reasons. They've had enough. Also included are people who yearn to do more fulfilling things with their precious time. They may already have a strong outside interest such as a small business venture, or a consuming hobby such as painting or photography.

Superficially, this group would seem right on course for an enjoyable and satisfying retirement. Dreams need to be based on reality, however, and sometimes people attempt to do too much too soon.

WHY ME?

These people feel as if the rug has been pulled out from under their feet. Their retirement may have come about earlier than expected, but this is not always so. Many who retire at 60 or 65 still have a sense of being pushed out, of the door being slammed in their face. They may feel that their work has not been sufficiently valued or appreciated. They may embark on their retirement with a feeling of resentment.

In this frame of mind, retirees may be likely to turn down any well-meaning ideas and suggestions supplied by friends or relatives. A failing to accept the present reality will only exacerbate it. While there is a certain emotional dividend in evoking sympathy and concern from relatives, such a negative attitude as this is harmful in the long run. Trying harder yourself can only be beneficial. It is just a matter of willing yourself to take the first steps towards independence.

WHATEVER SHALL I DO?

People in this group accept the inevitability of retirement quite graciously, but fail to get to grips with the new reality. They may not be used to taking initiatives. They may not fully recognise or appreciate the opportunities now before them.

There is a lot of potential for fulfilment here, but planning needs to start sooner rather than later. Once this group gets going, there may be no stopping them!

Our capacity for change

However broad the categories identified by retirement experts, no two individual sets of circumstances are ever the same. Factors such as your state of health and your domestic relationships are involved in your response to retirement. People's capacity for change varies, too. A person who has already shown an ability to adapt to changed circumstances, such as job changes, divorce, or remarriage, probably has the confidence of knowing they can cope. Someone who has been in the same job for years, living in the same house, and whose personal life has been unruffled, faces a far bigger challenge – the unknown.

Pre-retirement and retirement courses can help people to take a more objective look at their own lives, although, if only lasting a day or two, these may be too short to be really useful. Whatever your initial reactions to leaving full-time work, bear in mind that feelings change and mellow in the first year. Some people go through many phases of adjustment.

Tony, an architect, has an unambiguous response to retirement. He fits into the category of 'can't waits'. 'My job had become a joke – it was all about cost-cutting; nobody cared about standards any more. I began to wish more and more to produce something of worth, of value. For the last year or so of work, I used to cross off the sixth day of every month on the calendar; that's the date of my birthday, so it was one more step nearer retirement. In spite of that, there was an initial period after I first retired when I did suffer guilt – I felt I had to keep busy, to appease the gods as it were. Even now, I'll use the odd quarter of an hour or so while I'm waiting for the cooker timer to go off in order to practise the piano.'

Tony's interests include music – singing as well as playing the piano – and also watercolours. He believes that the most important third-age influence in his life is the memory of his mother. Not only did she learn the arts of embroidery and lace-making in her 60s, she reached such a high standard that she actually taught them for many years afterwards.

Few of us look to our parents as retirement role models. Many people in their generation were old before their time. They lived in the days when retirement was seen as a winding down, a putting out to grass. Nowadays that only applies to seaside donkeys.

For many people in the 1990s, retirement can be the start of a new phase of exploration and discovery. You are now your own boss, in charge of your own life. It's a big responsibility and it's all yours. Planning is essential. Without it, there's a tendency to potter, to make existing chores spin out to fill the time, and to be busy doing nothing in particular. Such a relaxed approach may be fine in the summer months when the good weather beckons and there's plenty to do. Dull days and the long winter months are a different matter. This is when planning counts. A programme of winter activities makes you get out and about when there's every excuse to stay at home.

Planning change

The exhortation to 'plan your retirement' sounds ambitious and rather formidable. It's true that responsible planning does include arranging your finances as much as you are able to, so that an adequate income is maintained in your later years. This is not an insignificant responsibility. Retirement, however, like any radical change in the pace and direction of your life, will also consist of a hundred and one *little* changes, all comparatively trivial in themselves. These lesser changes – some good, some not so good – need to be acknowledged so that you can find solutions and alternatives which will work in your favour, and not against you. Such changes are not difficult to plan.

In retirement it's often the little changes which affect people the most. Many people say how they miss the morning coffee break, especially in the first few months. They look at the clock and wonder what their former colleagues are talking about. People who live alone may have a particular need to replace this feeling of companionship. Meeting a friend, or inviting a neighbour in for coffee a couple of times a week, or sharing a regular pub lunch may be the answer. Don't wait to be asked; set up the arrangement yourself. Such meetings, however informal, may also provide the social pressure to dress up a little more smartly or to pay a visit to the hairdressers, etc. Many people miss the necessity of dressing for the office – 'it's so easy to let yourself go'. Building new networks of friends is the best way forward, and helps to address this problem.

New networks

Replacing the contacts of the workplace, business and social, requires a deliberate and conscious effort. Nevertheless it is important to keep in the mainstream of the outside world even though your perspective may have shifted. For many people the workplace provides a wide variety of contacts of different backgrounds and ages, and represents a cross-section of views and opinions. One reason why the attitudes of some elderly people can become narrowed is that they allow themselves to get cut off from everyday contact with other generations. They never have to confront a changing world. They can stay safely inside their shell. That way lies social isolation.

A network is any means whereby you meet other people. Networks are about opening doors, not closing them. They may be intergenerational or specifically for the over-50s. Don't spurn the latter: comparing notes, sharing experiences or just meeting with other retired people keeps you in touch with how others are coping with their changed lifestyle. This all acts as a valuable monitor to your own progress.

Local clubs, groups and societies are obvious examples of networks and these are discussed in Chapter 5.

Part-time employment

In early retirement many people are attracted to the idea of working part-time, for both social and financial reasons. The climate surrounding jobs for the over-50s is beginning to look brighter. Campaigning against age discrimination in job advertisements is becoming more widespread. Two major employment agencies have published forecast surveys for the 1990s pointing out the importance to employers of older workers and warning them against the blinkered ageist attitudes. Some employment agencies are setting up special divisions specialising in jobs for the older worker. One such agency which used to be called **Success after Sixty** has now changed its name to **Careers Continued** and has an office at 307–308 High Holborn, London WC1V 7LR. Tel: 071-831 9339.

Working patterns and attitudes to work vary enormously between individuals. For many men and women, work and retirement are all or nothing. They're often relieved to be rid of the strain of long-distance commuting, and only too pleased to have some time to themselves. However, if you are interested in the possibility of future work, be sure to inform your former employer. An ex-employee who may be security vetted will always be a more attractive proposition for seasonal or temporary assignments than unknown applicants.

So far, most of the employment initiatives offering prospects for older workers have come from the retail trade. Many customers prefer to be served by someone older who understands the value of customer service both in terms of a pleasant manner and knowing about the product. All the staff of the B&Q store in Macclesfield are aged over

50. Plus points for older workers in general are their loyalty and commitment, their common sense and reliability and their ability to get on with colleagues and customers.

In a healthy economy, opportunities for the over-50s should increase as employers abandon prejudices and confront the reality of a declining young workforce. They will increasingly need to find ways of attracting back older workers with a flexible programme of part-time and seasonal packages, job sharing, contracting out and, of course, retraining. The message from all this is clear.

Don't let any of your existing skills get rusty.

Don't miss any opportunity to acquire additional skills.

Don't neglect your health, fitness or appearance.

Try to be flexible and prepared for whatever new ventures may come your way.

Really serious job hunters will gain a lot of useful advice from an ACE Books publication called *Earning Money in Retirement* by Kenneth Lysons. There are tips on compiling a cv and covering letter as well as preparing for interviews, subtle skills which may have got rusty over the years but which are of paramount importance today. There is also advice on becoming self-employed, including working on a consultancy basis or taking out a franchise. The various implications of your tax status are also explained. (See pages 135–137 for further details about publications from ACE Books.)

Employment or work?

Employment isn't everything. Of course, a part-time or casual paid job can provide a structure to the week, but ideally the decision to take such a job will be from choice, not necessity. Does the job have enough flexibility not to crowd out the other opportunities that are open to you in retirement?

Employment should never be confused with work. For the first time in years, perhaps, you can now 'work' equally hard at your hobbies and interests. Cultivating a garden or allotment is certainly hard work; so is learning a new language or following a physical fitness programme. The fact that you're not paid for it in no way lessens your efforts. In fact, it is often the activities which keep you busiest that provide the greatest pleasure and satisfaction. Remember, you can now choose your activities and set your own pace. No one is at your back making unreasonable demands.

Retirement has sometimes been described as life's longest holiday, but who needs that? Some of the happiest retired people are the hardest working, and they would surely agree with George Bernard Shaw's assertion that a perpetual holiday is a working definition of hell!

CHAPTER TWO

Identifying your needs

When one door of happiness closes, another opens; but often we look so long at the closed door that we do not see the one which has been opened for us.

HELEN KELLER

Retirement is happening to thousands of people all the time. About 600,000 people retire each year; that's over 10,000 people each week. Nevertheless it's never happened to *you* before. You can read all the literature there is on the subject; you may prepare yourself by going on courses; but at the end of the day, your response is totally individual. Your feelings and reactions may be contradictory and surprising when the momentous day actually arrives. You may be able to share your thoughts with people who are close, or you may feel very much alone.

No two people's combination of health or domestic and financial circumstances are ever the same. However, airing and sharing experiences with others, whoever they are, will help you to come to terms with the change. Family and friends may be supportive and other social networks can be valuable too.

Be your own welfare department

When the workplace is left behind, home and community take on a new emphasis and importance. This may be nothing new for people who have spent most of their working lives juggling the responsibilities of these different contexts. For others, however, recognising and acknowledging the home as the new nerve centre may take time. Values and perspectives are very different, and so is the pace.

For some people, retirement may feel as strange as living in a foreign country. This isn't a bad analogy; at least the effort needed to adapt won't be underestimated! In the absence of an employer's welfare department, you now have to identify the problem areas yourself, and look for possible solutions. This means keeping up-to-date with information relevant to your age group and circumstances. Magazines are a useful way of doing this. The following retirement magazines contain regular articles on all aspects of health, leisure, pensions and benefits. *Choice* magazine is obtainable monthly over the counter in bookshops. For annual subscription details write to Choice Publications, Tower House, Sovereign Park, Market Harborough, Leicester-shire LE16 9EF. *Saga* magazine is available on subscription only. For details, contact Saga, Middelburg Square, Folkestone, Kent CT20 1AZ.

Solving the problems

The infinite variations surrounding an individual's retirement may throw up a number of problems. It's unwise to ignore areas of dissatisfaction in your life, in the hope that they will go away of their own accord. They rarely do, and solutions may be near at hand. Many such problems are rooted in the home, and precise circumstances will vary according to whether you are single or one half of a couple.

For singles

You may be facing retirement on your own because, like one in four of the general population, you live alone. This may have been a perfectly satisfactory situation when work absorbed five days of the week, but now that the day-to-day company of the workplace is missing, a single existence may get burdensome, especially when weekends no longer have any special significance.

People who live alone aren't necessarily loners. They may well have a network of family and friends not very far away. However, they may suffer from occasional loneliness, and need to make extra effort to compensate for the loss of colleagues.

Yvonne, *during a group discussion, happened to remark that she 'absolutely dreads' Sundays. She had lived alone quite happily since her divorce ten years before. It wasn't until she retired from nursing that Sundays became noticeably difficult. Her married daughter lived near by and, although she knew she was always welcome there, Yvonne felt that Sunday was the one day when her daughter and son-in-law could be together with their children. Yvonne could see her daughter and grandchildren any other day of the week.*

Yvonne's spontaneous comment about her Sunday doldrums caused an instant ripple of response amongst two or three other women in the group. Telephone numbers were exchanged and suggestions made to share Sunday lunch and occasional outings to exhibitions, galleries etc.

Some people miss frequent social contact more than others. Those whose jobs have involved dealing with people every day – such as sales representatives, teachers, nurses and shop workers – may miss the ebb and flow of changing faces, particularly if they live alone. Once they identify this particular need, they can take action to remedy the situation. One potential outlet is some sort of community/ volunteer work, where their highly developed social skills will be valued. Another possibility is to share their home from time to time, perhaps hosting foreign students on short courses.

For couples

People who live alone can make their own decisions and choices. For couples, retirement is a more complex issue involving communication and compromise if both halves are to feel happy and fulfilled. However, if one half has unrealistic expectations of the other, there is bound to be tension. For example, it is not uncommon to find people who, because *they* are retiring, automatically assume that their partner will also. This is not a promising start!

It is sometimes assumed that a man's retirement is more important than a woman's. For example, why is it that while the wives of male retirees are often invited to participate on company retirement courses, the husbands of female employees are usually ignored?

Since women's average earnings are less than men's, decisions about their jobs may take second place in family discussions. This can have bitter repercussions in retirement.

***Jane** had a part-time job in a solicitor's office which she very much enjoyed, along with the extra money she earned. When her husband retired, he made it clear that he wanted her company at home in the afternoons, and she resigned.*

'I didn't mind so much in the winter months, but when the spring came and he was out playing golf leaving me at home on my own, I really did feel resentful. There was an enormous row one day. He claimed he'd never insisted on my giving up my job, but he had made his feelings pretty clear. He admitted he'd never realised how much the job meant to me. I didn't even realise that myself until it wasn't there any more.'

Fortunately the story has a happy ending. Jane's former employer was more than pleased to have her back. Jane and her husband are now aware of the need for discussion, and not assumptions, in the future.

Retirement scenarios for couples will vary for many reasons, and according to whether one or both of you retire.

WHEN ONE OF YOU RETIRES

Even when it's just one of you that's retiring, you will both need to make considerable, individual adjustments. For example, a husband may be undergoing the transition into retirement with a partner who has not worked outside the home. Their respective adjustments will be very different.

Housewives don't retire: their domestic role continues, but under different circumstances. In fact, there may now be three meals a day to prepare instead of two! A woman may feel that her husband doesn't value her own right to freedom and leisure. In these circumstances, a reallocation of domestic chores is obviously called for, and will undoubtedly require tact and goodwill. Many partners are willing to make a belated effort to improve their domestic skills, but feeling they can never get it right is not much encouragement for a late beginner. One partner showing another how to cook is the equivalent of teaching him or her to drive. It's much better done by an uncritical outsider who isn't trying to score points. Ideally, a household where people are retired should have two active chefs and two practising drivers. In their leaflet *Advice for Older Drivers*, the AA stress that husband and wife should take an equal share of the driving, for both long and short journeys. Survival skills need plenty of practice if they are to be maintained.

Partners who are retiring around the same time will probably have already resolved the sharing of household tasks. Theoretically, retirement may seem like the beginning of a lifelong holiday together, but for two people who have led separate career lives, operating as a team may need practice. Priorities may sometimes clash (do they run two cars or learn to share one?). Both partners will need to undergo their own period of adjustment and balance their individual needs with togetherness.

It is realistic to assume that for any couple, however long they may have been together, starting to live under the same roof 24 hours a day is going to put a strain on their relationship. How they cope with the situation is a personal affair, but they may need some outside help. It's little wonder that the divorce rate for the over-60s is the second largest of any age group. Many couples could benefit from objective help with their changing relationship. Organisations like Relate (formerly the Marriage Guidance Council) or other forms of counselling play a vital role here. In the meantime, recognising that there may be difficulties is a good start. Common sense can go a very long way.

Widen your friendships

Many marriages become inward-looking, especially in retirement. Often, social contacts tend to be limited to old friends, frequently other married couples. This tends to make single people feel even more alone.

The fact that someone already has a constant companion is sometimes a disincentive to making new friendships – which is a pity. In the natural course of events, some of your old friends will move or fade away, and some will die. It's important to spread your friendships and use every available opportunity to make new friends. Otherwise, in time, you may lose the capacity to do this.

A husband and wife who have shared literally every activity and interest are ill-prepared for the future. One of them will ultimately feel very bereft when their partner dies and they are on their own. An inward-looking, self-contained marriage is a time-bomb for social isolation. How can you get to know new people who are likely to share your interests?

Companionship organisations

A big barrier to enjoying leisure activities is often the lack of a companion and a lack of confidence in trying something new on your own. A simple trip to the theatre or a restaurant is a lot less fun on your own.

Becoming a member of the Theatregoer's Club of Great Britain enables you to enjoy not only a variety of shows in the company of like-minded people from your own locality, but also a problem-free coach journey to the theatre and back. The scheme operates through 80 branches mainly in the south-east of England within reach of London's West End, where the problems of parking are most acute.

Members are mailed with regular details of a wide selection of shows, while local booking secretaries order the tickets and inform you of local pick-up points. In addition to the theatre trips there are outings to other places of interest.

An annual membership is payable, on top of the cost of tickets and coach travel. The seats are by no means the cheapest available, but the value of this arrangement lies in the comfort and companionship of a stress-free evening out. For the telephone number and address of your local booking secretary, contact the Theatregoer's Club of Great Britain, 55–56 St Martin's Lane, London WC2N 4EA.

WOMEN ONLY

Because there are substantially more older women than there are men, the absence of a companion is a predicament which affects them specifically. There are some useful organisations which have recognised the problem and offer a solution. They have all been started by individual women with first-hand experience of finding themselves alone. There is no guarantee of course that they can put you in touch with someone living near by: a lot will depend on chance. Please enclose a stamped addressed envelope when you write to them.

Contacts is a non-profit making social club for the over-50s. Members receive a list of members in their area, together with details of their hobbies and interests. The membership fee varies, depending on the number of members in your area; some areas are more active than others. For information, write to Contacts, 2 Knowle Close, Upper Woodcote Road, Caversham Heights, Reading, Berkshire RG4 7LH.

Focus 60, PO Box 394, London SW19 8QL, charges an annual membership fee which covers contacts with like-minded singles or couples as well as a regular newsletter.

Company has both a joining fee and an annual subscription. As well as a list of companions for social outings, it provides a service for pen friends, and for bed and breakfast in the UK. Its address is Evegate Park Barn, Evegate, Smeeth, Ashford, Kent.

Solitaire – Friends Indeed, PO Box 2, Hockley, Essex, requests a small voluntary donation. As well as an introduction to another member, it provides a pen friend service and a bed and breakfast list.

Holidays can pose particular problems for people on their own, such as the considerable additional expense of single supplements. Most of these organisations include a list of prospective holiday companions in their services. In addition to this, there is a specialist agency which deals exclusively with holidays, and takes a lot of care in matching people. For further information, write to **Travel Companions**, 110 High Mount, Station Road, London NW4 3ST. Tel: 081-202 8478.

Opportunities for women to appreciate privacy and space away from the home are rare. Older women in particular need to slip out of their traditional roles in order to discover new aspects of themselves.

The Hen House, a women's holiday and study centre in Lincolnshire, is a unique venture combining the services of a hotel with the informality of a country house. Here, women actively enjoy the company of other women. As well as short, creative courses on subjects such as music, dance and bodywork, there are a number of more introspective projects run by therapists and counsellors. For example, one course is aimed at helping single women to assert themselves, and another entitled 'Growing Old Disgracefully' is an enjoyable antidote to the stereotype of the older woman. More details are available from The Hen house, Hawerby Hall, North Thoresby, Lincolnshire DS36 5QL.

The Older Feminist's Network began in 1982 when many older women felt their needs and concerns were not being sufficiently represented within the more vocal women's movement. This informal open group gets together regularly in London, with many women travelling long distances to attend the meetings held on the second Saturday of each month, from 11.00am to 5.00pm at the Millman Community Rooms, Millman Street, 34–36 Alleyway, London WC1. For women who live too far away for a day trip, there is a newsletter. For more information contact The Older Feminist's Network, c/o 54 Gordon Road, London N3 1LP. Tel: 081-346 1900.

There is of course no reason why like-minded women in other towns and cities shouldn't start their own local informal network. The best way to find out if there are other interested people is to put up a notice in the local library. This is also the best place to enquire about local branches of self-help groups offering support in specific situations such as bereavement, separation or divorce.

MAINLY FOR MEN

Men have long enjoyed the freedom of their own predominantly male preserves such as clubs, pubs, rugby, football and cricket. Popular social venues for ex-service personnel, which embraces many people over the age of 55, are the clubs run by the Royal British Legion and other ex-service organisations. A neighbourhood new-comer, or someone on their own seeking social companionship, will be assured of meeting others with some degree of shared experience, even if this was confined to post-war National Service. Contact the Royal British Legion at 48 Pall Mall, London SW1Y 5JY. Tel: 071-973 0633.

For those who experienced active service, the camaraderie of the war years may be much missed. The Royal British Legion magazine, mailed free to all members, has a regular page with photographs called 'Lost Trails', where readers request up-to-date news of former comrades. *Saga* magazine (see p 23) also features this kind of column. Reunions do take place as a result of such contacts, and it's always good to hear from long-lost friends. A wise person, however, will understand that while it's pleasant to indulge in reminiscence occasionally, it's important to keep in touch and find a new role in the world of today.

The role you seek in retirement

There are certain pen and paper exercises which are designed to help people complete a self-assessment before making decisions about the rest of their lives. One suggestion is to write your own obituary! This may provide a stark reminder of interests and activities you wish to develop more fully. Another popular technique is to draw a horizontal line, not completely straight but with zig-zags or curves indicating the ups and downs in your life to date. These peaks and troughs may serve to remind you how you coped in past crises. Will the end of the line, your position at present, tail off upwards, signifying a positive optimistic view of the future?

Whichever way you choose to carry out your own personal audit, you should certainly include an MOT – a check on your physical health – to see what improvements can be made. Body maintenance is often a much-needed rescue job after years of inactivity, but fitness can be regained, as discussed in Chapter 6.

Retreats: a time for reflection

Major turning points in our lives, such as retirement, may encourage us to make a deeper response. We may feel the need to take stock and reflect. Our society is often preoccupied with the shallow and trivial, but there is no reason why we as individuals should not seek more meaningful experiences for ourselves. In recent decades there has been an increasing turning towards eastern religions with their practice of meditation and contemplation. There is, however, a long tradition of this within the Christian church in the form of retreats, a period of time consciously set aside for prayer, rest and spiritual regeneration.

A retreat can be for a day, a weekend, a week or a month. Some retreats are silent, others have themes and include creative activities such as painting or music. In many retreats time is set apart for personal interviews should you wish to talk over life problems.

Not all retreats are Catholic or Anglican, a few are Free Church, run by Methodists or Baptists. All of them welcome people from any denomination or those with no denominational allegiance, but who are comfortable in a Christian environment. Many retreat houses have drop-in days, which is a good way to acquire some appreciation of what is involved.

The National Retreat Association, a federation of retreat groups, publish a magazine called *Vision*, which includes an annual listing of retreats countrywide. You can send for more details to the National Retreat Association, Liddon House, 24 South Audley Street, London W1Y 5DL. Tel: 071-493 3534.

Write your own script

A particular professional group whose members don't tend to retire at any given age are actors. They tend to go on playing the roles of older men and women on stage and screen. The manner in which older people are portrayed in drama is a controversial issue. A frequent criticism is that most of the older characters are based on stereotypes. They tend to be crotchety, grouchy, clinging to outdated attitudes, resisting change, etc. Actors have little choice but to follow the lines they are given. It's different for you. Depending on the kind of role you want to play in your retirement, you can write your own script.

You may benefit from some background reading. A humorous starting point is *Many Happy Retirements*, a light-hearted publication from Age Exchange Theatre Trust, which comprises anecdotes from retired people themselves. It is available from Age Exchange Theatre Trust, 11 Blackheath Village, London SE3 9LA. Tel: 081-318 9105.

On a more serious note, the Open University (see p 60) publish a study pack entitled *Planning Retirement*, which consists of a book covering 60 topics from money matters to making new friends and an accompanying cassette, which develops these topics through interviews and discussions.

Finally, for some original thinking on the necessity for acknowledging change in the third age, try Charles Handy's *The Age of Unreason*, published by Hutchinson.

While background reading will help you to formulate viewpoints, self-analysis ultimately lies in the self. What are your goals? What are your priorities? Where do you start? It doesn't matter how simple and modest your aims might be, or how they appear to other people. Your goals should be valid and meaningful to *you*. Sometimes, a goal may be doing something new you've never done before, such as baking your own bread – an extremely satisfying and creative activity. Sometimes a goal comes into the category of second chances. Learning to swim is a typical example of an overdue childhood accomplishment successfully conquered somewhat late in the day by many older people. The significance of an achievement like this is totally personal. Perhaps having achieved your first set of goals, you may go on to face other more complicated challenges you'd never have dreamed of doing.

Going back to an earlier phase in your life is as good a start as any to finding new directions in retirement. Do you possess skills or talents which you have never fully developed or followed through? Now is the time to catch up, to explore and to experiment. There won't be another opportunity for freedom and creativity like this one.

CHAPTER THREE

Pursuits and pastimes

Absence of occupation is not rest,
A mind quite vacant is a mind distress'd.

WILLIAM COWPER

-B

The amount of time you have at your disposal in retirement encourages a tendency to potter about at your own pace. This is a wonderful contrast to the hectic existence you may have led at work, but the novelty wears off after a few months and you may find yourself being busy doing nothing at all. It's frighteningly easy to make existing activities expand and fill the available time. For many people, this kind of existence just isn't enough; it's like candyfloss, lacking in bite and substance.

Many retired people miss the goals and challenges of work; targets which require an increased effort and which, once achieved, are a considerable source of satisfaction. Having 50 extra hours each week at your disposal means that there is time to push yourself further. You can do more, and you can do it better. There are a number of exciting opportunities here.

You can raise existing skills and talents to a higher level.

You can maybe market these talents.

You can develop activities in such a way that they become more meaningful.

You can attempt something new and unfamiliar.

Masterclass mentality

Adopting a masterclass mentality, whereby you raise an existing skill or talent to a professional level or competition standard, can bring a great deal of personal satisfaction. An added reward is that you may now find yourself in a position to share your talent with others. For example, playing a musical instrument to a high standard enables you to entertain and bring pleasure to others.

Music-making

Many over-50s will remember piano or other music lessons as children, but how many ever kept it up beyond childhood?

Alec was a typical lapsed piano player until he retired from a lectureship in civil engineering. He then felt he'd like to take it up again. Just to be sure that this feeling wasn't going to be a ten-day wonder, he first bought himself an electronic keyboard in order to check that his brain and his fingers would still be in harmony after all these years.

After three months he was confident that he definitely wanted to go back to the piano, so he sold the keyboard and bought one. A couple of years later, when Alec was an active member of his local U3A (see p 52), he had the idea of getting together with others to share music-making. He put a notice in the U3A newsletter to ask if any other piano-playing members would be interested in playing solos and duets at each other's homes. Within a couple of months there were ten other piano players, most of them around Grade 5 standard, which Alec describes as the point at which most pianists have the ability to play for others.

'What I didn't foresee was that, as well as the motivation for coming and enjoying the meetings, there is the added stimulus of wanting to practise again because of the opportunity to play in front of people. Playing the piano on your own at home can be a lonely business.'

Already Alec's church has suggested he play at occasional services. Although he has never taken any examinations before, he will soon be taking Grade 5. He's now talking about going further and perhaps ultimately teaching the subject.

The time-consuming business of learning or improving one's skills on a musical instrument is an ideal occupation in retirement. Pianos and most other instruments are available on short-term hire, a useful option for those who wish to test their aptitude and application. Your local music shop is a good source of information and may be able to recommend local teachers. Music teachers sometimes advertise in the local paper or on noticeboards in the library. Your library should also have an up-to-date copy of the Register of Professional Private Music Teachers, published by the Incorporated Society of Musicians. This covers most instruments and includes singing teachers. Also in the library will be details of all musical activities taking place at arts centres or in local halls and churches.

Singing

Many over-50s will have sung in school or church choirs and, although this may have been a long time ago, it can come as a shock to realise we can't sing like we used to. This is hardly surprising. The voice is produced by a set of muscles in the throat and, like any muscles, they need regular exercise if they are to work properly. Few people are tone deaf; what most of them lack is confidence and practice.

Any singing group run by the local adult education service (see p 51) will probably start with warm-up vocal exercises consisting of la-la-ing and humming, in addition to relaxation and breathing exercises. Once you know how, you can do these exercises at home and your voice will gain in strength.

Local singing groups and choirs vary enormously, both in what and how they sing. For some choirs you are required to audition, and need to be able to sight-read. However, singing for fun is often a part of other club's activities. Christmas carol concerts and other singing events are often part of fundraising activities for many ventures, and just joining in on this level may give you the right balance between rehearsal, achievement and fun.

Market your talents

Not everybody is musical. Many people are very clever with their hands. With the additional time that retirement brings, you may wish to learn or develop a craft. Crafts are currently enjoying a revival of interest and, provided your work is of a high standard, there may even be the possibility of earning money from your hobby. Marketable craft skills include antique furniture restoration, picture framing, hand and machine knitting, dressmaking, and cake decorating as well as catering for weddings and other functions. If there is a big enough demand, you might develop the activity to the level of a small business, in which case you would need to seek out some professional advice. The Age Concern publication *Earning Money in Retirement* may be useful background reading (details on p 135). There is also the possibility of teaching your skills to others, for which you would need the appropriate qualification, eg a City & Guilds or Royal Society of Arts certificate. In very many cases, however, it's not the money that matters but the knowledge that your ability is recognised.

Develop your interests

Language learning

The interest which you managed to sustain in the evenings or at weekends while you were working, can now blossom with the extra investments of time and energy you are able to make. This should increase your knowledge of the subject in both its breadth and depth. For example, if you have managed to maintain your French, you could now broaden your interest and improve your skills by doing any of the following:

- listening to French radio programmes;
- reading French newspapers;
- being a holiday host to French students;
- taking an *en famille* holiday yourself in the home of a French family;
- arranging a home-exchange holiday;
- renting a *gîte* for a self-catering holiday.

An agency which specialises in arranging family stays for people of all ages, either as individuals or couples, is En Famille Overseas. They find host families in various European countries, but mostly in France – in towns and cities, in the country and by the sea. Visits can be arranged at any time of the year for any length of stay, from a week to a year.

Dorothy, *a widow from Merseyside, has enjoyed seven such holidays with her friend Gwen, another widow, whom she met at her first French class some years ago. 'We'd been learning French together, so we thought why not go on a holiday and make use of it?'*

Dorothy admits she was very nervous the first time, mainly coping with the language and staying with a strange family. 'It's not like a hotel. You've got to fit in with the rest of the family.'

Now, Dorothy says she actually reads more French than English. 'We've both been rewarded to find that in our 60s we could still rise to the challenge.'

For further information, write to En Famille Overseas, The Old Stables, 60b Maltravers Street, Arundel, West Sussex BN18 9BG. Tel: 0903 883266.

Gardening

Gardening, one of the most popular hobbies in retirement, is another interest which is ripe for development! There are many aspects of gardening other than tending your own little patch.

VISITS

You can enjoy a pleasant day out and learn a lot when you visit places like the Royal Botanical Gardens at Kew, the Royal Horticultural Society's Gardens at Wisley, and Ryton Gardens, the National Centre for Organic Gardening, which is at Ryton-on-Dunsmore, Coventry CV8 3LG. Tel: 0203 303517. The Museum of Garden History, run by the Tradescant Trust at St Mary-at-Lambeth, Lambeth Palace Road, London SE1 7JU. Tel: 071-261 1891, is another interesting place to visit.

An annual publication from the National Garden Scheme lists private and public gardens which are open on certain days of the year in aid of charity. Teas are usually provided and there are often plants for sale. *Gardens of England and Wales*, or the Yellow Book as it's more commonly known, is available through booksellers or by post from the National Gardens Scheme, Hatchlands Park, East Clandon, Guildford, Surrey GU4 7RT. Tel: 0483 211535.

DEMONSTRATIONS AND LECTURES

The Royal Horticultural Society (RHS) have a programme of regular lectures and demonstrations at each of their various locations: Wisley (Surrey), Pershore (Worcestershire), Rosemoor (Devon), and Harrogate and Ness Gardens (Cheshire). These are advertised in the RHS Journal and are open to non-members as well as members.

Horticultural Therapy, an organisation which encourages older and disabled people to get involved in practical gardening, run regular demonstration workshops and meetings. There is advice on specially adapted tools, and members receive a quarterly magazine. More information can be obtained from Horticultural Therapy, Goulds Ground, Vallis Way, Frome, Somerset BA11 3DW. Tel: 0373 464782.

COMPETITIONS AND SHOWS

You can, of course, join your local horticultural society and enter their annual show. Should you already be one of Britain's estimated 250,000 allotment holders, you could enter for the National Allotment Competition organised every year by the *Daily Mirror* newspaper. The judges are less concerned about giant marrows than they are with the allotment as a working unit. A recent, first time, 58-year-old winner gained crucial extra points by being the only entrant in his area to pass the garden shed test with flying colours. He was the only competitor able to produce a fully stocked first aid kit!

Try something new

Raising and developing the skills and talents we possess is an understandable goal in retirement. We already have a foundation on which to build. But what about the unknown? With 50 full and shining hours at our disposal each week, there is plenty of time to mix old activities with something new.

It may be tempting to opt for the familiar, the tried and true, but it doesn't take a great deal of effort. To attempt something completely new requires a lot of courage, especially in later life when the rest of the world expects us to sit back and rest on our laurels.

Absolute beginners

No one really knows what they're capable of until they actually try. It's never too late to start from zero. That is the philosophy behind the Dark Horse Venture, a nationwide scheme to encourage older people to discover hidden talents and untried skills.

The Dark Horse Venture is rather like a Duke of Edinburgh Award scheme for seniors; in fact, Dark Horse Vice-Chairwoman, Pearl Clark, has used much of her professional administrative experience with the Duke of Edinburgh Award Scheme as background to the Venture. Chairwoman, Mary Thomas, who pioneered the Dark Horse Venture in Liverpool, gave it that title because, as she says, 'everyone is one'.

To join the Venture you have to be over 55 and take up an activity you have not previously attempted. Your first task is to find someone to teach and guide you for a year. You and your teacher agree on a target, and when you have achieved it you apply for your award. There are no exams and no comparisons; what you are aiming for is your own personal best. Awards are given within three categories:

- Giving and sharing, which means being involved with and offering assistance to others in the community.
- Learning and doing, which includes individual or group hobbies.
- Exploring and exercising, which comprises travel, exploration or physical recreation.

Every activity you could think of is covered by these three categories. Practical examples include learning Russian, word processing, lace making, playing the cello, writing books, Outward Bound courses, and even tap dancing. It was in tap dancing that ageism reared its ugly head. In one area of the country several dancing schools insisted that older people could not do tap dancing – only ballroom dancing. Three dark horses went on to prove them wrong!

Peggy is a widow in her 70s. For her first Dark Horse project she kept a diary of her garden, month by month, in which she recorded the seasonal changes with photographs, paintings and pressed flowers. She also kept a second album, in which she listed her many and varied plants. Her assessor was a public parks head ranger, and Peggy freely acknowledges the amount of information she gained from him concerning the names and history of her garden plants. Had it not been for the Dark Horse assignment, she doubts whether she would have started, let alone completed such a task. Now she has a wonderful memento of a year in the life of her garden to keep for years to come, as well as the Dark horse certificate she was awarded. The story doesn't end there. Attempting to grow bonsai trees was Peggy's next venture, which in turn led to pottery classes in order to make little bonsai pots. Her next target was less horticultural in nature; she learnt to play the steel drums under the guidance of a musician from Trinidad. She and a friend have already played at a Christmas concert.

You can join the Dark Horse Venture either on your own or as part of a group. For a leaflet and more information contact the Dark Horse Venture, Kelton, Woodlands Road, Liverpool L17 0AN. Tel: 051-729 0092.

Writing for publication

Many people have a secret ambition to see their work in print, but it may not be until they are retired that there is sufficient time to get down to the actual business of writing.

What is it that you want to write and who do you want to write for? You may wish to experiment in different directions. Within the field of fiction alone the range is enormous: novels, drama and short stories – for adults as well as children. Remember, Mary Wesley's first novel was published when she was 70, while a later novel, *The Camomile Lawn*, has been dramatised on television. Non-fiction includes autobiography, books on special subjects, travel books, and articles for newspapers and magazines. Or perhaps your interest lies in poetry.

It is likely that your writing preference is reflected in your own reading. Certainly, if you are aiming at publication, it is vital to read as much other published work as possible in your chosen area. This performs several useful functions. First, it helps to compare your own writing with published work. Does it measure up? Reading round your area may also guide you to a gap in the market and will certainly help you to avoid duplication. Finally, this kind of research will guide you to the publishers who specialise in your field.

USEFUL GUIDANCE

Creative writing classes and study groups are run by adult education classes (see p 51), branches of the Workers' Educational Association and University of the Third Age groups (see p 52). Residential courses for writers are widely advertised in literary magazines or as special interest holidays. You will need to do some research to find a course which matches your needs, experience and aspirations. In addition, there are local writers' circles and workshops, where members of all ages provide mutual support and encouragement. Your library should have addresses and telephone numbers for those in your area.

You may prefer to work on your writing privately; it is a lonely pursuit after all, and you may wish to rely on your own assessment of your work. A home study course run by the National Extension College (see p 59) may interest you. There is also a magazine called *Writers News* specifically produced for new writers and which gives details of the many awards and competitions open to both previously published and unpublished writers. For subscription rates write to *Writers News*, FREEPOST, PO Box 4, Nairn, IV12 4BR. Tel: 0667 5441.

The Book Trust publish a *Guide to Literary Prizes, Grants and Awards*, obtainable from the Publications Department, The Book Trust, Book House, 45 East Hill, London SW18 2QZ. Tel: 081-870 9055. Also obtainable are some notes for guidance called *Getting Published*, which include basic advice on how to present a manuscript and find a publisher, together with a useful bibliography. The notes are free, but please enclose a large stamped addressed envelope.

Finally, another useful publication is the *Writers' and Artists' Handbook*, published annually by A & C Black and available in most libraries.

ALTERNATIVE PUBLISHING

Many small publishing outlets have set themselves up over the last 20 years in order to produce a different kind of writing to that represented by mainstream publishers. Such outlets may be a more likely possibility for certain kinds of writing, such as personal reminiscence, which interests many older writers. An interesting, well-written autobiography, local history project, or collection of poetry may be accepted for publication by a community publisher, or a publishing cooperative linked to a community or arts centre. Alternatively, you might like to contact your Regional Arts Association, who will have someone who is responsible for encouraging writing projects. Ask at your local library for the address, or write to the Arts Council, 14 Great Peter Street, London SW1P 3NQ. Tel: 071-333 0100.

Poetry is a specialised area. There are possibilities of individual poems being published in poetry magazines or through competitions. A list of these can be obtained from the Poetry Library, South Bank Centre, Royal Festival Hall, London SE1 8XX. Please enclose a large stamped addressed envelope.

Whatever kind of writing you pursue, beware the vanity publisher. This is the name given to a firm which offers to publish work of would-be authors for a fee. Although this may be a tempting proposition, it can result in a hefty bill. Vanity publishing is not to be confused with self publishing, which may be a successful outlet for a specialised book. With self publishing, you are not only responsible for writing the material, but also for the editing, design, marketing and selling functions, probably by mail order from your own home. Your considerable input includes the financial backing, and researching (and paying) the printer of your choice.

Self publishing produces some useful and attractive books which, perhaps in view of their minority interest, are unlikely to find favour with mainstream publishers. However, they involve a considerable amount of expertise and expense and are an unwise choice for the interested amateur.

Hang on to your pastimes

Although making the most of your abilities and reaching high standards is a valid and honourable aim, it is the activity itself and not the end result which provides individual satisfaction. High achievers sometimes find it difficult to settle for less when time catches up with them and perhaps affects their eyesight and dexterity. They may even feel that if they can't do it properly, then they won't do it at all – the perfect excuse for not starting anything in the first place!

Keep up with your pursuits and pastimes for as long as you can; these interests are your lifeline. When people stop performing the precious skills that have occupied them over the years there may be little to replace them.

Ellen remembers her mother, who cooked the family meals until well into her 80s in spite of failing eyesight. One day her mother mistook the salt for the sugar, and ruined the supper as a result. She was bitterly upset about this, and vowed she would never cook again. Consequently, her role as a participating family member disappeared and Ellen observed that she began to feel worthless and depressed. A recognition that her eyesight was diminishing, together with a more effective labelling system in the kitchen, might have avoided this painful outcome.

This everyday story of domestic life is an extreme example, but is echoed a thousand times by much younger retired people who relinquish a hobby or pastime prematurely and them suffer withdrawal symptoms in the years that follow. Don't let the colour and quality of your creative life be weakened without first making an effort to confront the dragon.

Older people, who may be experiencing annoying physical limitations for the first time, rarely think of themselves as being disabled. *'Tempus fugit'* is how they often ruefully refer to frustrating physical restrictions, such as arthritic fingers which no longer hold a paintbrush steady. You may well find a solution to your individual difficulty if you consult one of the many organisations which cater for the needs of disabled people. There is a positive emphasis nowadays on promoting and encouraging leisure and creative activities.

If deteriorating sight is a problem, the Partially Sighted Society may be able to help. They have a print enlarging service which is useful for recipes and knitting patterns, as well as sheet music. Contact them at The Partially Sighted Society, Queens Road, Doncaster, South Yorkshire DN1 2NX. Tel: 0302 323132.

With a little ingenuity, you can usually find a way around most problems. A catalogue called *Simple Solutions*, available free of charge from Age Concern's Marketing Department, contains a variety of useful items, eg:

- long handled gardening tools which save bending;
- needlework aids including a sewing machine needle threader and a knitting needle holder which enables you to knit with one arm;
- easy grip gadgets for pens and pencils to make writing easier;
- kitchen gadgets designed to cope with a weak grip or shaky hands.

If you have a specific problem to which you are unable to find a ready answer, then telephone or write to the Information Service of the Disabled Living Foundation, 380–384 Harrow Road, London W9 2HU. Tel: 071-289 6111. The more details you can give them, the more successful they may be in helping you. The Foundation also publish a reference book, *The DLF Information Service Handbook*, covering all aspects of disabled living needs. The section dealing with leisure activities can be bought separately from the above address. Alternatively, you may find a copy in your local library.

Occasionally, the only answer may be to lower your expectations in line with your capabilities. You might have to settle for painting in watercolours rather than drawing freehand. Alternatively, you might look for a variation in a pastime which has become too arduous. For example, instead of maintaining a garden you might prefer to run a greenhouse where the work is less physical and involves little bending, as well as being protected from the weather.

Striking a sensible balance is a necessary survival skill. Compromise is *not* the same as giving up, so long as the limitations come from outside and not from within.

CHAPTER FOUR

Learning opportunities

Education is not the filling of a pail,
but the lighting of a fire.

WILLIAM BUTLER YEATS

The ways and means of expanding mental and creative horizons are vast and varied, and there are no age limits. No two adult learners ever start out from precisely the same spot, which is why, according to tutors, adult teaching is so much more interesting than working with children. Adult students are constantly surprising their teachers. Everyone over the age of 50 has picked up innumerable bits and pieces of knowledge along the way. Experience, together with a lifetime's background reading, counts for so much. People are often far better educated than they realise, in spite of maybe having missed out on paper qualifications. Sadly, many older people considerably underestimate their potential for intellectual and artistic development, not to mention achievement.

What are you looking for?

People learn in different ways. Some are attracted to a formal, structured learning plan, with courses and examinations. Others prefer to wander and explore more informally, setting their own pace. Sometimes it isn't always clear in your own mind what exactly it is you are looking for, and you are aware only of a feeling of restlessness and curiosity for all those books you haven't read, the languages you can't speak, places you've never visited and paintings you've never seen.

Why do you want to study? Is it for your own personal satisfaction, for fun, or really seriously? These aims aren't mutually exclusive, and you may be motivated by all three. People's reason for study varies from individual to individual.

- You may want to refresh and continue previous study from years ago.
- You may be looking for stimulating and mind-stretching ways of passing the time in the congenial company of like-minded people. The subject choice may be less important than the social aspect of sharing common interests and concerns.
- You may want to update typing skills by following a course on word processing or computer studies.

- You may wish to acquire a practical skill like car maintenance.
- You may simply wish to find out more about a subject that interests you.

Factors affecting your choice

Your own motivation and preferences apart, other crucial factors are involved in your proposed choice of study. Classes are provided by a range of sources – some of which are statutory, some voluntary. The range and availability of day and evening classes on offer will depend on where you live. It may also depend on, for example, the priority which your local authority gives to adult education. Classes are more expensive now, and some local authorities have chosen to cut their adult classes quite drastically. They are also extremely cost conscious when planning new classes. However, as payers of local council taxes, older members of the community have as much right as anyone to influence decisions about local services, such as education. There have been many examples throughout thee country where groups of older learners have successfully lobbied against cuts in adult education. It is vital to keep your local councillors informed if you feel they haven't got their priorities right.

Local transport facilities are another important factor. Unless you can reach your weekly class without undue difficulty in the winter months, regular attendance is bound to be affected. If your local adult education classes are uninspiring or inaccessible, you may wish to consider short residential courses. They are ideal for those who would welcome and can afford a change of scene. Similarly, more and more people are now opting for the extra dimension and stimulation offered by so-called 'special interest' holidays. These can be anything from light hobby breaks to weightier residential courses, usually in comfortable accommodation in beautiful surroundings at home or abroad.

For more serious, on-going study, 'distance learning' courses are available via the National Extension College, the Open University, and the Open College of the Arts. All these options are fully described in the following pages. However, for the less fully committed there is a valuable education resource which is easily available and accessible to all, regardless of where you live, and that is broadcasting by the radio and television networks.

Radio and television

Most broadcasting companies aim to educate, inform and entertain, and, of course, there's no reason why an educational programme shouldn't also prove popular, and vice versa! The 'Antiques Road-show', 'Tomorrow's World' and wildlife films are all examples of programmes which are informative and interesting to a wide audience. High quality publications often accompany these and many other series, such as those on cookery, health and gardening, and together they form a congenial context for learning.

Language learning is a prime example of educational broadcasting at its best. These days a foreign language is invariably taught alongside a country's popular culture. Television is particularly good at doing this. In addition to programmes, there may be cassettes, videos and books to accompany language series, which are often transmitted on Sunday mornings.

Since there's nothing more annoying than missing a programme which interests you, it's well worth doing an occasional trawl of television and radio listings in order to make a note of promising-sounding programmes. Obtaining advance notice of forthcoming educational programmes is possible if you write direct to the individual companies. For BBC programmes contact BBC Education Information, BBC White City, London W12 7TS. Tel: 081-746 1111.

The Independent Television Commission used to provide a mailing list service alerting viewers to educational programmes on ITV and Channel 4, but unfortunately this will shortly be discontinued. However, each regional television franchise holder has a community education officer to whom you should write for advance information. For Channel 4 programmes viewers should write to Derek Jones,

Editor, Support Services, Channel 4, 60 Charlotte Street, London W1P 2AX.

A recent development at Channel 4 has been the formation of Channel 4 Clubs; to date Gardening and Science clubs. Both clubs produce newsletters, giving members advance notice of programmes and accompanying booklets, which are available at a discount. There are plans to launch an Arts Club and possibly others, too. For membership details of existing clubs, write to PO Box 4000, Cardiff CF5 2XT.

Attending classes near your home

Three different organisations supply a wide range of day and evening classes.

The Adult Education Service

The Workers' Educational Association

The University of the Third Age

Adult Education Service

These classes are run by your local authority. They begin in September each year and follow the academic year, with breaks at half-term, Christmas and Easter, and a long break during the summer months. In addition to year-long courses there may also be short six-week courses, or occasional Saturday courses, run as taster sessions for subjects such as pottery, calligraphy, yoga, etc.

A prospectus of all courses in your area is produced by mid-August, and copies are either distributed on a house-to-house basis or are freely available at your local library.

Classes on offer cover academic, vocational, physical and practical subjects, and might include cookery, photography, dressmaking, machine knitting, English Literature, computer studies, keep fit – the variety is impressive. Subjects are taught at different levels; beginners, intermediate and advanced. A language class, for example, might have as its title 'Spanish for your holiday' which distinguishes it from a more orthodox language course leading to graded examinations. Cookery classes often have a range of themes: vegetarian or microwave cooking, or cooking for one.

Enrolment for courses is in early September, in person on set days, or by post. Some adult education services even accept telephone bookings from credit card holders. Gone are the days of long queues in the rain.

If you are in any doubt about the content or level of an advertised course, you can obtain more precise information from the local college, whose telephone number will be in the prospectus. Fees for courses vary in different parts of the country but there are usually reductions for pensioners.

Workers' Educational Association

The Workers' Educational Association (WEA) is another national provider of day and evening classes in a wide range of subjects. There are nearly a thousand branches in Great Britain, and you can obtain the address of your local branch from the library or local authority education office. WEA classes tend to be rather more academic and intellectual in content than those run by the local authority adult education service. Tutors are usually university lecturers who may ask for written essays and reading between classes. Fees for courses vary according to the amount of subsidy available, and retired people should enquire about reductions. Fellow students will be of mixed ages and from all walks of life. The WEA also run residential courses. For more information, write to WEA, 17 Victoria Park Square, Bethnal Green, London E2 9PB. Tel: 081-983 1515.

The University of the Third Age

Some 23,000 members belong to the University of the Third Age (U3A). The 'university' label is misleading; no qualifications, diplomas, degrees or exams are involved. The people who join their local U3A group simply value the opportunity to share and exchange views on a wide range of topics – not all of them academic; on the lighter side there may be bridge, Scrabble, rambles and outings to local places of interest. Each local U3A develops in response to the needs and resources of its own area. All the activities are arranged by the members themselves who share the organisation and administration.

One of the advantages of the U3A study groups is that they can start at any time of the year and are on-going. They don't have to fit in with the timetable of the academic year. Providing there is room in a group, a new member can join straightaway, instead of having to wait until the new term of the following September, as is the case with other adult education classes. Some groups have no long break in the summer, which will be another advantage for those who miss the stimulus such meetings provide. There are financial advantages, too. Apart from an annual membership fee and possibly a contribution to room hire, the fee for study groups is very modest or may even be free. Members offer their services and experience without payment.

A potential disadvantage with U3A study groups is that since membership consists exclusively of retired people, there is no contact with younger students. Additionally, newly-established groups may suffer at first from a lack of people who are confident and willing to lead a group. Since many group leaders are former lecturers and teachers, it can take some time before members with no teaching background feel sufficiently confident to set up a study group in an academic subject. For U3A groups to work successfully, members have got be willing to participate in the fullest sense of the word. However, further generalisations are impossible, since so much depends on individual members.

As a form of social contact U3A also has much to recommend it. At a national level, it publishes a termly newspaper called *Third Age News*. There is a Travel Club through which members organise special interest holidays for small parties, as well as house-swap and paying-guest lists. Subject networks currently link members around the country who are interested in languages, oral history and creative writing.

A list of names and addresses of countrywide U3As is available on receipt of a large stamped addressed envelope from U3A National Office, 1 Stockwell Green, London SW9 9JF. Tel: 071-737 2541. If there is no U3A in your area, you can become a national individual associate for a small fee per annum which entitles you to copies of the newspaper and to make use of the travel facilities.

Local museums and galleries

If you live within reasonable distance of any major gallery or museum, you have an additional learning resource on your doorstep. Many of them now provide a pre-recorded telephone service giving opening times, along with the dates and admission charges for any special exhibitions.

Not so widely known is the work of museum education departments, which besides catering for schools, also provide a programme of courses, lectures and events for interested adults. There may also be a programme of outings and events organised exclusively for 'friends' of the museum, whose annual subscriptions support the museum and its activities. The Victoria and Albert Museum and the National Maritime Museum in London are examples of institutions offering this kind of facility.

Away from home

Many people are either unable or unwilling to commit themselves to an on-going course. Extended trips away may mean missing a whole term's classes. A useful alternative, therefore, is the short, residential course where you 'throw yourself' into a subject or activity for a short, concentrated period of time. Providing you are able to afford the fees, which of course include food and accommodation, these courses can be extremely refreshing. They are also a good way of 'tasting' an activity like dinghy sailing, for example, to see whether you like it, and gaining a measure of expertise quite quickly. You might then have the confidence to pursue the activity from home.

The choice of residential courses on offer is extensive. They vary in their duration, their intentions, and the activities and subjects on offer, as well as according to the kind of accommodation they provide and the participants they hope to attract. Take your time in choosing the course which best suits you. There are three main types.

Special interest holidays

Summer schools

Study breaks

Special interest holidays

Hobby or theme holidays, leisure learning breaks, special interest holidays – whatever the title, this kind of holiday combines a stay in a pleasant hotel with some form of light study activity as the main attraction. The break may last a week or a fortnight, although some hotel chains have short special interest weekends. Typical themes include antiques, bridge, whist, gardening, etc and there is often a celebrity expert who acts as host. Brochures and leaflets for these kinds of holidays can be found in travel agents. Alternatively write to the English Tourist Board, Thames Tower, Blacks Road, London W6 9EL. Tel: 081-846 9000.

Saga, the travel firm for the over-60s, also specialise in this kind of break, and their range of topics includes music and opera. Bear in mind, however, that with Saga, fellow holiday-makers will all be in the retirement age range. It's up to you whether you welcome this in your fellow guests or whether you would prefer the opportunity to meet a wider range of people. One of the fascinations of a hobby can be the huge diversity of individuals it attracts – people who otherwise may have little in common. Saga do not use travel agents; contact them at Saga Holidays Ltd, FREEPOST, Folkestone, Kent CT20 1AZ.

Summer schools

For truly intergenerational study holidays, some independent boarding schools, notably Millfield and Taunton schools in Somerset, run summer schools in July and August. Look out for the wide range of advertisements for these kind of schools in the national press, particularly at weekends. Summer schools offer a range of week-long activities for all ages from children over seven. Programmes vary from year to year but typical examples of adult subjects are classes in studying antiques, the modern novel, local history, or the wines of Europe. Grown-ups can improve their golf, bridge, or painting and drawing skills, while children can try cooking, sport activities or arts and crafts.

This kind of holiday break could be ideal for a family get-together, with everyone doing their own thing during the day and meeting up for dinner in the evening. Free brochures are available from Millfield School Village of Education, Street, Somerset BA16 0YD. Tel: 0458 45823 and Taunton Summer School, Taunton School, Taunton, Somerset TA2 6AD. Tel: 0823 276543.

You can send for a copy of the Summer Schools Supplement from Independent Schools Information Service, 56 Buckingham Gate, London SW1E 6AG.

Summer schools are also run by universities, who wish to make use of their excellent facilities during the long summer break. Summer Academy is a consortium of universities offering one-week courses in subjects such as history, literature and natural history, with visits to local features such as churches, monasteries or Hadrian's Wall. The consortium comprises Stirling, Swansea, Sheffield, Liverpool, East Anglia, Exeter, Southampton, Kent and durham. *Summer Academy Study Holidays* is a free publication giving full details about the courses on offer. You can obtain it by writing to Summer Academy, School of Continuing Education, The University, Canterbury CT2 7NX. Tel: 0227 470402.

Study breaks

There are literally hundreds of residential study breaks on offer during the course of the year at all kinds of colleges, schools and field study centres around the country. Course providers include colleges which belong to the Adult Residential Colleges Association (ARCA), and many of these are based in large country houses in superb settings. Field study centres and places like Coleg Harlech in the Snowdonia National Park offer courses for the great outdoors; Brighton Polytechnic Language Centre offers intensive one-week language courses. There are courses held in potteries, a music trust which introduces people to chamber music, orchestral works or jazz; and many opportunities for painting and drawing of all kinds.

Many students come on their own to attend these courses. Quite apart from the fascinating variety of subjects on offer, study breaks are one solution to the problem of holidaying on your own, experienced by many retired people who are single.

The definitive guide to residential study breaks, both in the UK and abroad, is a publication called *Time to Learn*, published twice a year by the National Institute for Adult Continuing Education. The January edition gives details of courses from April to September; the August edition covers October to March. It is available in bookshops or can be obtained from the National Institute of Adult Continuing Education, 19B De Montfort Street, Leicester LE1 7GE. Tel: 0533 551451. Those colleges which have easy access and facilities for disabled students are marked with a symbol.

More sustained study

There must be many retired people today who look back with regret on missed opportunities, particularly people whose early or subsequent education was interrupted by the war years. If you've enjoyed attending day or evening classes and gained confidence as a result, you may like to consider the idea of more sustained study. Alternatively, you may feel your education has been one-sided, with perhaps an over-emphasis on science or the arts, and would welcome an opportunity to redress the balance.

Attending a course

If you live near a university, polytechnic or other higher or further education college, you may wish to enrol on one of the many courses they offer. Mature students are welcomed, and are sometimes accepted on the basis of past experience rather than the paper qualifications demanded of school-leavers. If you are accepted for a degree course, you may be eligible for a grant from the local authority to cover the cost of tuition fees, provided that you have never had one before. Many local authorities offer an educational guidance service for adults.

Universities and colleges often have lively extra-mural departments which run short courses with no entry requirement. Write to the department direct to obtain a full prospectus.

Distance learning

For many retired would-be students, correspondence courses or distance learning offers a far greater flexibility in the choice of courses. Correspondence colleges are widely advertised in newspapers and magazines and often hold out the promise of qualifications. How do you know if such courses are worth the fees, or the qualifications worth the paper they are written on? You can check credentials with the Council for the Accreditation of Correspondence Colleges who monitor such courses and provide a list of recognised colleges. Their address is 27 Marylebone Road, London NW1 5JS. Tel: 071-935 5391.

All three of the main and most widely-known providers of distance-learning courses have a high proportion of older students. These are:

The National Extension College

The Open University

The Open College of the Arts

The distance learning offered by these three providers has many advantages.

- There are no age restrictions, entry qualifications or preliminary admission interviews.

- Where you live is unimportant. All course material, consisting of specially produced books, audio and video cassettes, is sent to you through the post. Similarly, you send your assignments to your tutor by post.

- You study at the time which suits you; six to seven hours per week is an average minimum.

- You are able to select your courses according to your personal goals. You don't have to take exams if you don't wish to. You can take a break between courses should you wish to travel for a month or two, or take time off for any other reason.

- Although you do not form part of a class, you are not isolated. You are supported by a tutor/counsellor who is assigned to you, and there are also opportunities to meet other students.

- You can start many courses as soon as you apply, without having to wait until the beginning of the academic year.

THE NATIONAL EXTENSION COLLEGE

The National Extension College (NEC) is an educational trust offering a wide range of home study courses including GCSE and A-level courses, as well as the opportunity to take these exams if and when you choose.

Many older students left school without qualifications, and for those who would like to try out a subject at GCSE level before committing themselves to a full exam course, the NEC offer an option called 'A Taste of GCSE', available in any of seven subjects. Similarly, for the many would-be older students who lack confidence in their study skills, there are helpful courses on 'How to Study Effectively' and 'How to Write Essays'.

Margaret, unlike some other older NEC students, already had a degree, as well as teaching experience in Religious Education and Geography. However, like many people in this country, Margaret felt herself to be scientifically illiterate and so she enrolled on two NEC courses, 'Preparing for Technology' and 'The World of Science'. That was some time ago. Since then, Margaret has taken no fewer than nine NEC courses including A-level Maths and GCSE electronics. 'Quite honestly, I got hooked,' says Margaret. She went on to study with the Open University (for which NEC courses are a recommended preparation) and is now doing an Environmental Science degree course at the University of East Anglia. When Margaret first began studying with the NEC, it was to increase her understanding of the sciences. Now she wishes to help others do the same and hopes to become a tutor for the NEC or Open University.

Not all NEC courses are academic in nature. Some are geared towards hobbies, eg 'Birds and Birdwatching', and there are courses on counselling and business skills. Fees for all courses can be paid in instalments and there is a discount for those on low incomes. For more details, write to the National Extension College, 18 Brooklands Avenue, Cambridge CB2 2HN. Tel: 0223 316644.

THE OPEN UNIVERSITY

The Open University (OU) runs separate programmes. The first comprises the BA degree courses for which the OU is renowned. The second comprises Community Education courses for those who prefer a shorter form of study relevant to everyday life. There is also a leisure series.

Admission to OU degree courses is made on a 'first come, first served' basis. The demand for places usually exceeds the places available, so there may well be a waiting list. The OU aims for a balance of students on arts/social science and maths/science/technology courses, and discriminates in favour of disabled applicants by offering guaranteed admission.

All new undergraduates receive a preparatory package before their course begins, in order to ensure that OU study really is for them. Similarly, in the first year there is a choice of foundation courses which assume little previous knowledge and help to develop the learning skills which will be necessary for the higher level course that follows.

Your ultimate degree is based on the number of credits which are acquired on the completion of a course. You need six credits for an ordinary degree, eight for an Honours degree. Degrees can be made up of various combinations of courses. Choices are left as flexible as possible, and you don't have to decide a long way ahead.

A week's residential summer school is part of each course. The total cost of obtaining an ordinary degree would be between £2000–£3000, usually spread over four to six years. OU students do not qualify for the mandatory local authority grants which are available for conventional university or college courses, but there may be other help available, as a booklet on financial support explains. For example, your local authority might agree to pay the fees for your summer school.

The OU's Community Education courses consist of study packs suitable for individual or group study. Courses can be started at any time, and include 'Retirement Planning' and 'Living in a Changing Society'.

The Leisure series of courses consist of multi-media resource packs, details of which are contained in a separate leaflet. There are no set time scales, essays or assignments. Subject choices cover art, music, women's writing and computing.

To obtain more information about the OU, you might visit one of its 13 regional centres, which provide a service for enquirers. These are the principal source of personal advice for potential students, and provide an opportunity to look at study material first hand. The address and telephone number of your nearest regional centre may be listed in the telephone directory under 'Open University'. Otherwise contact the Central Enquiry Service, The Open University, PO Box 200, Milton Keynes MK7 6YZ. Tel: 0908 274066.

THE OPEN COLLEGE OF THE ARTS

The Open College of the Arts, an educational trust, aims to provide a home-based education in the arts along similar lines to the Open University, although not quite as flexible. For many courses, including those in Art and Design, Painting, Sculpture, Garden Design, Music and Textiles, you are required to attend group tutorials at a regional centre every three weeks or so, in addition to home study. Other courses, eg those in Photography, Creative Writing and Understanding Western Art, are taught by correspondence only, backed up by postal tutorial support and you can begin them at any time of the year.

Since much of the work is practical and creative, many students choose to repeat the same year's course for a second year and there are reduced rates for those who do this. Students can go on to do a second, third and fourth year in some subjects. Some students opt for assessment of their work, while others do it for their own satisfaction. As with the Open University, there are no admission qualifications, and as yet there are no recognised awards or qualifications for completing an Open College of the Arts course. The course organiser for Painting, Sculpture and Textiles is Ian Simpson, former Principal at St Martin's School of Art. He comments, 'I start from the premise that anyone can learn to paint. It's a natural means of expression which all children do well and which most people stop doing because they believe painting is a "gift" which needs a special kind of talent. Painting can reveal imaginative and creative powers that you didn't know you possessed, and enables you to become aware of the marvellous richness of colour and patterns that is everywhere.'

For more information, write to the Open College of the Arts, FREEPOST, Barnsley S70 6BR. Tel: 0226 730495.

CHAPTER FIVE

Community involvement

When you cease to make a contribution you begin to die.

ELEANOR ROOSEVELT

Community involvement is a term which covers a huge range of possibilities for participation; for example, campaigning on behalf of a cause, joining a club or society, or working as a volunteer. These activities are not mutually exclusive; indeed the objectives behind them may often overlap. While some people choose to devote all their time and energy to one favoured cause, others prefer to divide them between a range of activities which perhaps reflect different interests in their personal life.

Participating in the life of your community can greatly ease the transition from full-time work into retirement. It can help to build a new identity which is valid for today. Rather than defining yourself in terms of the past – 'I used to be a teacher/civil servant/architect/ nursing sister, etc', you can now define yourself in terms of the present – 'I'm a counsellor with the Citizens' Advice Bureau' or 'I'm on our local heritage conservation committee' or 'I work with the theatre and arts association'. It is then immediately apparent to everyone that you are living in the present. Socially, this is deeply reassuring to both you and others. It makes it so much easier, for example, to strike up a conversation with someone you have only just met.

Discovering a new role for yourself doesn't happen overnight, however. It may take a while to find yourself the right niche. There may even be a couple of false starts: opportunities which prove disappointing and insufficiently challenging. Be patient and keep working at it. It's not a full diary you're aiming for, but a full and satisfying life.

Get to know your neighbourhood

When people retire, they frequently admit they haven't a clue about what is happening on their own doorstep. There is usually a very good reason for this. For example, many people work a long way from the place where they live, leaving the house each day before eight, and not returning until seven at night. Little wonder that they are not active in local affairs.

Newcomers to an area often seem to know far more about what's going on locally than long-standing residents. The reason is simple: newcomers make a conscious effort to meet people and to discover the facilities which interest them most. Now that you are retired, you need to survey your local area with fresh eyes, no matter how long you have lived there. Your perspective has changed. You need links with the local community in order to meet and mix with other people. What's more, your local community needs you.

In the first instance, you will perhaps be seeking new interests and activities for the daytime. Remember, however, that while you were working full-time, you may have limited evening activities because of the need to get up early for work the next morning. Now, if you have the energy and inclination, you can commit yourself more widely.

A prime source of information on local activities is your public library, where you will find leaflets and notices on a wide range of clubs and societies, along with the names and addresses of the organisers. This kind of information may be on display, or it may be kept in the reference section. Don't hesitate to ask library staff if you need their assistance to find something specific – they are there to help.

Local newspapers will also contain regular club listings, giving the times and venues. There may be interesting news or feature stories; the activities of environmental groups are particularly newsworthy these days.

Clubs, groups and societies

What will suit you?

You will want to know a lot more than just the time and place before committing yourself to membership of a club or society. It should be possible to attend an initial meeting as a guest, and to ask for a copy of the forthcoming programme. With a history society, for example, the list of invited speakers will be a good indication of the level at which the society is pitched. If the club is creative – drama, art or photography, for example – you will wish to know what sort of standard is expected. Are beginners welcome? Will other members share their skills or do they work quite independently of each other? These are perfectly legitimate questions to ask any club secretary, though there are other ways of conducting research. Local art societies frequently hold exhibitions of their members' work, and attending these will tell you a lot about the standards achieved. Similarly, if drama or music groups appeal to you, you would be well-advised to attend local performances and judge where you might fit it. Standards will obviously vary, and you may have to audition.

High standards and prestige performances aren't everything, of course, and behind the scenes there may be bad feeling and jealousy about who gets the leading roles, etc. You will only really discover what the atmosphere in a club is like by talking candidly to members, and most probably by a process of trial and error.

One reason why it's useful to look round carefully before committing yourself to a club is because you may find the same activity performed by a different group in a manner which is much more to your liking. For example, many community-based arts and theatre projects rely on a team of willing helpers in order to keep going. So, if it's theatre which interests you, instead of joining your local amateur dramatic group, you might be able to join a project where professionals and amateurs collaborate as a team. The Brewhouse Theatre and Arts Centre in Taunton, for example, operates with a paid staff of nine, and a team of 400 volunteers! Volunteers carry out a range of jobs for which they receive appropriate training. They help out in the box office; they sell programmes and refreshments; backstage they act as dressers, scenery shifters, and light and sound operators. The catering department is an important revenue-earner for the whole arts centre. Much of the food in the cafe is prepared at home by volunteers who are reimbursed for the cost of ingredients, and who serve it at lunchtime.

Employers' retirement groups

Large countrywide employers such as the civil service and the National Health Service have their own retirement fellowships with local branches. Some companies run social clubs for former employees.

Initially you may feel a certain hesitation in joining this kind of 'pensioners' club', either because of the activities or because you feel so many of the existing members may be years older than you, with little in common. Do give it a try and at least keep your options open with a nominal membership, which will entitle you to copies of newsletters, magazines, invitations to Christmas lunches, etc. You might consider more active membership later on when you have met other members who, like yourself, feel a natural resistance to being categorised with an ageist label. An alternative approach would be to offer your services to help organise the entertainments and outings. There is a very useful free publication for anyone with this responsibility called *Coaches Welcome*. The booklet includes a county by county guide to museums, stately homes, theme parks, etc together with their opening hours and parking facilities. For a free copy write to C W Circulation, Lewis Productions Ltd, Unit 3, River Gardens Business Centre, Spur Road, Feltham, Middlesex TW14 0SN.

In addition to outings, there is usually a need for active members willing to take on a welfare role, visiting members who are housebound or in hospital.

ARP Over 50

The Association of Retired Persons (ARP) recently amalgamated with the Over-50 club. For a modest membership fee members receive the quarterly magazine and discounts on a range of goods and services, as well as access to telephone helplines offering legal advice and assistance in finding reputable help for domestic emergencies. Friendship centres are run on a voluntary basis by members themselves, organising the hire of a local hall and holding meetings once a month.

One of the aims of ARP Over 50 is to change public attitudes towards ageing. They have an employment service, Age Works, which is linked to the French employment agency Ecco.

For further information write to ARP Over 50, Third Floor, Greencoat House, Francis Street, London SW1P 1DZ. Tel:071-895 8880/3.

Women's clubs

Some of the long-standing national women's organisations continue to enjoy enormous popularity. The National Federation of Women's Institutes report that many new members join them for the first time at retirement age. Women's Institutes (WIs) are by no means exclusive to rural areas and you will find them in towns and cities, where members perhaps take a more progressive stance on, for example, women's issues or the environment. Newcomers are often wary of the 'jam and Jerusalem' image, like the woman who commented, 'I thought the WI was all cakes and apple pies until my neighbour dragged me along to an evening on nuclear power!' Meetings consist of talks, demonstrations and discussions and there are opportunities for training and participation in public speaking. The WI also run courses on setting up small businesses, and have a marketing shops division. A residential college offers a wide range of short courses on all subjects, including computer studies.

Your local library will have details of your local WI. In cases of difficulty, however, you should contact the National Federation of Women's Institutes, 104 New Kings Road, London SW6 4LY. Tel: 071-371 9300. The Scottish equivalent of the WI is the Scottish Women's Rural Institutes, 42 Heriot Row, Edinburgh EH3 6ES. Tel: 031-225 1724.

Townswomen's Guilds also attract many new members at retirement age. There are around 2000 guilds throughout the country, each holding its own regular meetings, at a time which reflects the needs of the local membership. Again, your local library should have all the details about meeting times and venues. In case of difficulty, contact the national organisation's head office at Townswomen's Guilds, Chamber of Commerce House, 75 Harborne Road, Birmingham B15 3DA. Tel: 021-456 3435.

Age Concern groups

Fit and active retired 55-year-olds are rarely immediately attracted to their local Age Concern. Most groups cater more for elderly, less mobile pensioners. There are exceptions, however, one of which is Leicester Age Concern, one of the biggest and most innovative in the country. Activities here include desktop publishing, creative writing and yoga, to name but a few. There is a library, hairdressing salon, and chiropody facilities as well as a restaurant. Work opportunities, provided by a trust, include dressmaking alterations and hand-knitting. Such sophisticated services have been made possible through sponsorship and links with local business firms.

More Age Concern groups are becoming aware of the importance of enjoyable and health-promoting activities such as keep fit, indoor bowls and swimming. Local groups are often a useful source of information concerning activities in the area for the over-50s, even if they don't offer these themselves. Retired people with spare time on their hands are always welcome as volunteers.

Finding your own level

You need to find a level of community participation with which you feel comfortable. It isn't always easy for someone who has enjoyed a managerial position in a hierarchical organisation to adjust to being on a par with fellow volunteers or committee members. Some chiefs are happy to be Indians; others find it another difficult adjustment demanded of them in retirement. If, for example, you've been involved in public relations, you may find yourself increasingly irritated by what you perceive as the dabbling amateurism of your society's publicity officer. In the context of a local committee, your professional skills may be seen as a threat rather than an asset and your presence may be resented. Sensitivity is called for. There is sometimes friction on committees which have been dominated by the same post holders over the years. Try to be tolerant and relaxed; change is more easily effected when people don't feel threatened.

Don't let pettiness get in the way of something you really want to do. If, on the other hand, you really feel like a fish out of water in your local set-up, then you may get more satisfaction further afield by offering your services to a bigger organisation in the wider community.

Sometimes retirement activities which are totally unrelated to your former job work out the best. Retired accountants, for example, get fed-up being continually asked to be treasurer of this and that organisation. Often it's more tempting to try out activities which draw on other facets of your personality. Many people have no great need for status; it enough to know their efforts are needed and their contribution appreciated. The pianist who plays the accompaniment for the weekly keep-fit class, or who leads the sing-along at the day centre; the driver of the minibus who takes local disabled youngsters to the sports centre, or housebound elderly people to the luncheon club; these people are valuable facilitators, enabling others to participate fully in the life of the community.

Outdoor activities

Most people spend the bulk of their working lives indoors, often office-bound. It's no surprise, then, that many see retirement as an opportunity to redress this. You can combine a wish to spend more time outdoors *and* participate in your local community by joining one of the many environmental groups which have recently grown in both size and number.

Such groups are flourishing, and actively attracting members from all age groups. They may have a particular appeal for older people who remember the countryside of their childhood and may feel a strong commitment to preserving what is left for the sake of future generations.

Many groups are associated with national organisations, for example Friends of the Earth, who have 330 groups countrywide. Local activities will vary. If you live in a town or city, there will be more emphasis on monitoring projects, measuring pollution, and campaigning for recycling facilities. If you live within easy reach of open spaces, the priority of your local group will probably be the practical preservation and protection of wildlife and the countryside. You can contact Friends of the Earth at 26–28 Underwood Street, London N1 7JQ. Tel: 071-490 1555. Many other groups and trusts are doing similar work, and publicise themselves at the library or in local newspapers.

The Ramblers' Association encourage and preserve the people's right of access to the countryside. Around 300 local groups go on regular walks, keeping footpaths open and accessible to the public. This is a congenial way to get to know people. The head office of the Ramblers' Association is 1–5 Wandsworth Road, London SW8 2XX. Tel: 071-582 6878.

Woodland preservation. This is a particularly high priority in the West Sussex area where various trusts and conservation groups cooperate in volunteer schemes. One volunteer team, the West Dean Woods Nature Reserve Volunteers, consists of around 30 active elders, who won a national Age Resource Award for their conservation work in West Dean Woods, a 38-acre site north of Chichester. When woodland becomes overgrown, many species of flora and fauna gradually disappear. Thanks to the cutting, clearing and new planting carried out by these older volunteers, West Dean Woods is once again home to about 30 kinds of birds, butterflies and wild flowers.

Woodland skills, such as coppicing, are demonstrated and taught in projects run by the British Trust for Conservation Volunteers, who have 750 local groups countrywide. The Trust also organise working holidays, and – provided you are reasonably fit – there are opportunities to spend a working break away from home, learning and practising country skills like hedging and dry stone walling. Enquiries about local groups or the summer programme of working holidays should be sent to BTCV, 36 St Mary's Street, Wallingford, Oxfordshire OX10 0EU. Tel: 0491 39766.

Scottish Conservation Projects (SCP) also offer breaks lasting a weekend, a week or a fortnight when volunteer members can help with wood clearing and creating nature trails. Individual skills such as chain-sawing are also taught on weekend courses. Write to Scottish Conservation Projects, Balallan House, 24 Allam Park, Stirling FK8 2QG. Tel: 0786 79697.

There are also opportunities for practical voluntary work on bird reserves through membership of the Royal Society for the Protection of Birds. You might also join one of their 750 local groups. No membership is necessary in order to encourage your own garden wildlife! A wide variety of bird species can be attracted simply by the correct siting of appropriate bird feeders stocked with particular foods. The RSPB sell a range of bird feeders and provide helpful advice on how to build nesting boxes, and encourage birds into your garden. Write to them at the Royal Society for the Protection of Birds, The Lodge, Sandy, Bedfordshire SG19 2DL. Tel: 0767 680551.

Communicating with others

Helping visitors

If your part of the world happens to be on the tourist map, there are often vacancies for volunteer stewards and curators in museums and heritage centres. The National Trust, for example, rely heavily on volunteers to issue tickets, sell booklets and souvenirs, and answer visitors' questions. They also need practical help with conservation jobs such as the re-wiring of old buildings. Enquiries should be made locally or to the National Trust, Heywood House, Westbury, Wiltshire BA13 4NA. Tel: 0373 826826.

Volunteers provide information and guidance in many of the national and city museums and art galleries, stately homes, cathedrals and so on. You may be interested in joining a group of 'Friends' who support an individual institution by raising funds, and planning special events and activities.

There are often personal reasons why someone is drawn to a particular volunteer post.

Colette is a volunteer curator at the Stanley Spencer Gallery in Cookham on the River Thames, where the painter was born and spent *most of his working life. Indeed, Colette's late husband had known him.*

The gallery contains a permanent but changing collection of paintings, Spencer's letters and other memorabilia. Colette herself went to art school in Hammersmith some years ago and makes regular visits to the London galleries. She is therefore well qualified to answer visitors' queries.

Another of Colette's interests revolves around the twinning of Marlow, her home town, with Marly Le Roi, near Paris. Colette speaks fluent French and has enjoyed staying with local people on her visits to Marly. Every other year or so, she reciprocates by offering hospitality to visitors from Marly.

Town twinning: a European outlook

The idea of twinning UK towns and villages with counterpart communities in Europe originated at the end of the Second World War. The EC now plans to boost these links with the help of a European Twinning Fund. A twinning relationship is usually set up by the local authority, which then assists and encourages local groups to arrange their own exchanges and visits. Such groups might include scouts or guides, women's clubs, or retirement groups, and the links could be based on sport, trade, music or drama. Travel concessions are usually available from ferries and airlines.

A video about town twinning, called *A Citizen's Europe* is available for hire from the Twinning Section, Local Government International Bureau, 35 Great Smith Street, London SW1P 3BJ. Tel: 071-222 1636. This agency arranges the twinnings on behalf of local authorities. It is possible that your town already has a European twin, in which case you should ask at your town hall or council offices for information about related local activities.

Corresponding with prisoners

One group of people prevented from any sort of community participation are those detained in prison. When the Prison Reform Trust discovered a need particularly amongst long-serving prisoners for penfriends in the outside world, they set up a correspondence scheme with a number of recommended guidelines; for example, the Trust acts as a go-between so an individual correspondent's home address is never used.

If you are interested in the idea of corresponding with a prisoner, write initially to the Prison Reform Trust giving some idea of your background and interests so that these can be matched with a penfriend on the inside. Letters may be sent by individuals, or written as a group activity, by a class of schoolchildren, for example. Censorship only applies to Category A, high-security prisoners, so your letters are private. If you wish to find out more about the scheme, write to the Penfriends Scheme, Prison Reform Trust, 59 Caledonian Road, London N6 9BU. Tel: 071-278 9815.

Opportunities for volunteers

Community participation enhances the quality of life for very many retired people. Becoming a volunteer is a natural outlet for someone with time and energy to spare. Unfortunately, the term 'voluntary work' has a ring of do-goodism about it. It sounds so patronising and, sadly, deters many people who are non-judgmental in attitude and don't divide the world into 'us' and 'them'.

In practical terms, of course, there is little difference between supporting a pressure group, being an active club member , or being some kind of volunteer. All these activities can be challenging and enjoyable and may replace many of the positive aspects of a former job. They also require time, energy and commitment.

Recent research conducted for the Volunteer Centre uncovered three interesting points.

- Most people become volunteers by accident, because a friend or relative asked them to.
- The main reason why more people are not volunteers is because no one has ever asked them.

- The main reason why people drop out of volunteering is because of the way organisations manage their volunteers; there may be exploitation, amateurism and a lack of training and support.

There are important lessons here for voluntary organisations, but these three points are also very good reasons why retired people in search of fulfilment need to take matters into their own hands. There is no shortage of vacancies, but choosing the right volunteer placement is as important as finding the right job. It won't come about by chance. As a mature person, you know that your retirement is your own responsibility. You will need to find out as much as you can before taking on a volunteer post, so that you can make informed choices in the light of your priorities.

Where to look

The following sources will provide you with some idea of the range of volunteer vacancies in your area.

- The local library, where there are often leaflets and notices from agencies seeking volunteers.
- A volunteer bureau, set up to match people to jobs. Check under 'Volunteer' in your local telephone directory.
- Your local hospital may have a volunteer coordinator or a 'Friends' organisation whose members usually run the hospital shop.
- Local branches of national organisations such as British Red Cross, Samaritans, Age Concern, etc.
- Specialist volunteer agencies such as REACH or RSVP (see p 79).

What's involved?

Before even seeking a volunteer placement, it will help you to draw up a cv. This cv will not be quite like those you have prepared for job applications in the past, but it is along similar lines. The purpose of this cv is to remind yourself of any specific skills and human qualities you have, which are not necessarily applicable in the workplace, but are relevant and valuable when dealing with others in a volunteer role. Your personal cv might include such plus points as:

- an ability to listen;
- empathy and/or experience with a particular age group, eg elderly people, children, teenagers;
- personal experience of stressful situations, eg looking after a disabled or elderly relative, divorce, bereavement;
- practical skills and experience, eg driving, office work;
- creative skills such as playing a musical instrument, or a knowledge of crafts or painting.

Far from being a waste of time, this exercise will help you select a voluntary post more likely to provide you with job satisfaction. Collating these strands of experience will also be of value in your application and interview.

Voluntary work for a helping agency involves a serious commitment; without it, vulnerable people may suffer. This is one reason why potential volunteers are usually expected to go through a selection and interview procedure, followed by a training course. Training is an expense for agencies, which is why they need to be reasonably sure of your reliability and staying power before accepting you. Additionally, there are some tasks, counselling in particular, where the requirements and confidentiality of the job are exceptionally rigorous.

You may be turned down, either at selection or interview stage. You should be given a tactful but honest reason. This may seem like a slap in the face at the time, but don't let it get you down. There are plenty of other opportunities with other organisations. Have a re-think and try again somewhere else.

Beware of ageism

Arbitrary age limits are nonsense for most things. In any group of individuals there are enormous variations in health, energy, outlook, motivation and life experience. However, age discrimination *does* exist in the voluntary sector; it is almost as rife as in the wider world of paid employment. Indeed, what makes it worse in the voluntary sector is that it is an issue which is often swept under the carpet.

When voluntary organisations appeal for volunteers, they obviously don't advertise the fact that they have age limits. Some are currently reviewing their outdated policies. Voluntary Service Overseas (VSO) recently increased their age ceiling from 65 to 70 years. In many cases, existing volunteers are not necessarily asked to stand down when they reach the organisation's 'sell-by date', but first-time volunteers are not accepted. The usual excuse is that the cost of training would outweigh the agency's return in length of service. This does not bear close scrutiny. People drop out of volunteering for various reasons at all ages. An older person suffering from chronic ill health is hardly likely to be seeking voluntary work. The more likely candidate is a person who feels fit enough for the job and has energy to spare. Charitable organisations do sometimes have difficulties, however, in obtaining insurance cover for older volunteers, particularly if driving is involved.

A whole chapter is devoted to voluntary organisations and their age limits in *Age: The Unrecognised Discrimination*, an ACE Books publication. Lessons for the active older would-be volunteer are clear.

- Don't leave this sphere of activity too late.
- If you are turned down because of an arbitrary age limit, then let the world know. Write to your local newspaper, local councillor, MP, Age Concern, etc. Voluntary organisations which have such age limits should declare them openly, so that their actions can be publicly challenged.

Where life experience counts

Volunteers are sometimes drawn to a particular agency for reasons which are entirely personal. An individual experience of bereavement may motivate some people to offer their support to others via a bereavement project. CRUSE – Bereavement Care is the national organisation for bereavement care, providing counselling, practical help and social events through its many local branches. They use volunteers at a local level and can be contacted at 126 Sheen Road, Richmond, Surrey TW9 1UR. Tel: 081-940 4818.

Hospital Information Points (HIPs) are run by Arthritis Care and located in certain rheumatology clinics. They are staffed by volunteers, many of whom suffer from this painful condition themselves. HIPs are there to tell other patients about local meetings and publications, as well as the information and advice service available from Arthritis Care, 18 Stephenson Way, London NW1 2HD. Tel: 071-916 1500.

The Stroke Association (formerly known as the Chest, Heart and Stroke Association) run a nationwide Volunteer Stroke Scheme whereby volunteers visit speech-impaired patients in their own homes to help with activities to stimulate the memory, telling the time, handling money, word games and puzzles. The aim is to slowly build up the patient's confidence and to encourage motivation. People who have experienced, at first- or second-hand, the debilitating effects of a stroke form a considerable number of VSS volunteers. Details can be obtained from The Stroke Association, CHSA House, Whitecross Street, London EC1 8JJ. Tel: 071-490 7999.

Specialist volunteer agencies

Men and women who have enjoyed a particularly challenging and demanding career often wish to put their professional expertise at the service of others. There is a nationwide agency called the Retired Executives Action Clearing House (REACH) which finds part-time, expenses-only jobs for retired people in a wide range of voluntary organisations seeking professional help. Many of the jobs are short-term and offer the stimulus of work without the long hours or on-going pressures. A countrywide team of 'matchers' links the right person with the right job.

Ann was Business Administrator for BUPA and found herself getting bored in her retirement. REACH arranged an introduction to the Aldershot branch of SAAFA, the Soldiers', Sailors' and Airmen's Families Association, just prior to the Gulf War. Ann and colleagues liaised with local services to create a 24-hour Gulf support centre, one of the first of a countrywide network.

There is a video available which relates the experience of other REACH placements. Write for further details to REACH, 89 Southwark Street, London SE1 0HD. Tel: 071-928 0452.

With the Retired Senior Volunteer Programme (RSVP), volunteers work together as a team on whatever local community project they have chosen. It may be assisting in a school, or working in a hospital as ward befrienders. In Bristol an RSVP team does a regular 'blood run', collecting and delivering specimens to three local hospitals.

At a primary school in Cambridge, volunteers keen on gardening asked the local garden centre for packets of unsold seeds. They then showed the children how to prepare and plant seed trays and how to raise seedlings. Together they prepared the waste ground around the school for the young plants.

RSVP has a lot to offer the older volunteer. Not only do you get back-up support and the satisfaction that you are doing a useful job, but you also have the companionship of people in your own age group. It may not be operating in your area as yet, in which case enquiries should be made to RSVP, 237 Pentonville Road, London N1 9NJ. Tel: 071-278 6601.

If you are a good organiser and like taking the initiative, you may like to approach the New Horizons Trust. Grants of up to £5,000 are available to groups of retired people wishing to start their own community projects. There should be at least ten people in your group, half of whom should be over 60. Projects should aim to improve local amenities or to fill existing gaps in social provision. A leaflet with all the details is available from New Horizons Trust, Paramount House, 290–292 Brighton Road, South Croydon, Surrey CR2 6AG. Tel: 081-686 0201.

Campaigning for your rights

In this country there are dozens of pensioner organisations all involved in campaigning for increased state pensions, older people's access to educational facilities, travel concessions and better geriatric health care under the NHS. Write to Age Concern England for a Briefing on Pensioner Organisations, enclosing a large stamped addressed envelope. Whatever their shade of political opinion, older people need to make their voices heard and feel their views matter. Just because you happen to be retired doesn't mean you're unconcerned about children's education, job training for young people or any other issue affecting other groups in society. Maggie Kuhn, leader of the Gray Panther Movement in America, provided sound advice for British third-agers when she said, 'Don't cut yourselves off from the rest of society by being just a special interest group. Involve yourselves in intergenerational issues; in co-operative ventures, not competitive ones.'

There is a lot to be said for remaining or becoming active members of mainstream organisations, be they pressure groups or political parties at a national or local level. That way, the point of view of your generation is not sidelined, but is heard and considered as part of a whole.

Don't become invisible just because you've retired. You have more spare time now to write letters to your MP or to editors of newspapers and magazines, and to let them know your feelings on topical issues. Similarly, on the domestic front, don't hesitate to complain if goods or services aren't to your liking. Many causes for complaint are echoed and shared by others who have less spare time than you in which to take action. The Consumer Association has a useful book called *120 Letters that Get Results* (obtainable from Dept MBSA, PO Box 44, Hertford SG14 1LH) which includes a whole section on how to complain about services provided by the NHS.

CHAPTER SIX

Exercising body and mind

If you watch a game, it's fun.
If you play it, it's recreation.
If you work at it, it's golf.

BOB HOPE

Physical and mental activity are never two completely different functions. Mind and body can't be separated so easily. While you're exercising one, you are automatically bending and stretching the other. A dance or keep-fit routine involves memory and concentration; many sports require judgement and coordination. What we should be looking for in retirement is a balance which takes into account individual preferences and choices but which doesn't reflect one aspect of self at the expense of another.

Many men and women in retirement need body maintenance as a rescue job. They need to recover from years of neglect. Their mind, however, has probably kept active through work. Most thinking people recognise the need for mental stimulus in the years ahead far more readily than they do the physical effort to keep in shape. We all need a gentle push in the right direction.

Why physical fitness matters

For most retired people it is usually the years of inactivity, rather than ageing, which causes the deterioration in physical fitness. The good news is that fitness can be regained. Almost everybody over the age of 50, however sedentary and whatever their health problems, can benefit from exercise, providing it is gentle and safe. You should also enjoy it, of course! Progress may be slow and improvements may take time, but the result will be a feeling of well-being which will make the effort worthwhile and encourage you to continue. Wouldn't it be nice not to puff every time you have to walk uphill or climb a flight of stairs? There are many advantages in maintaining regular exercise in later life.

- It helps you keep supple and prevents stiffness in your spine and joints. Particular arthritis-prone areas are knees, shoulders, hips and fingers.
- It maintains muscle strength, which makes it easier to cope with everyday jobs like weeding the garden, cleaning windows, carrying shopping, etc.

- It contributes to keeping your weight under control.
- It assists stamina so that you can eventually take part in more sustained and sociable sporting activities, such as bowling, table tennis, hill walking, etc.
- It helps prevent osteoporosis in women, especially through weight-bearing activities.
- It will increase your confidence and self-esteem by making you feel better and look better.

Research from the United States amongst older car drivers has shown that those who take regular exercise often retain alertness and coordination and are able to carry on driving until a greater age than those drivers who don't.

You can perform suitable exercise at home to the accompaniment of a cassette, video or keep-fit programme on television. Joining a class is probably more fun.

Keep-fit classes

Keep-fit classes for the over-50s (which also includes the over-60s, 70s and 80s) are available at most sports and leisure centres, regardless of whether these are run privately or by the local authority. Keep-fit classes for the older age group are also listed in the prospectus produced by your local adult education service. These classes are fee-paying but there are usually concessions for retired people. However, you will have to pay the whole course fee in advance, whether you miss a class or not. The advantage of keep-fit classes which take place in church halls, usually advertised locally, is that you pay by the session. They may also be within walking distance of home. Don't be unduly influenced by the premises. What matters is the quality of class leadership and the general group atmosphere. Is it a friendly and relaxed class to go to?

A likely source of keep-fit activities for men is the local YMCA, which will be listed in the Yellow Pages. If there is any kind of keep-fit programme it will usually include sessions for the over-50s at very reasonable charges.

Extend is an educational charity which specialises in movement to music classes for the older age group. Many of the exercises are performed sitting on chairs, at least in the early stages. You can write to them to see if there is a class near you at Extend, 1A North Street, Sheringham, Norfolk NR26 8LJ. Please enclose a stamped addressed envelope. Also try the Keep-Fit Association, 16 Upper Woburn Place, London WC1H 0QG. Tel: 071-387 4349. Both Extend and Keep-Fit Association teachers are specially trained to work with older people.

Dance to fitness

Most keep-fit classes nowadays are performed to music; sometimes it's a piano, but more often it's disco music with a strong beat which certainly gets everyone moving. As a contrast, you may like to try a more flowing type of movement to music called Medau; classes are often featured in adult education brochures.

With any kind of dancing you are exercising without realising it. The range is limitless. You shouldn't have any difficulty in finding classes in any of the following: ballroom, sequence, country, Scottish or even tap dancing. Perhaps a little more elusive but growing in popularity is circle dancing, based on folk dances from Greece and the Balkans, which is often performed out of doors.

Some warnings

The usual advice to retired people with a health problem or who haven't done any exercise for some time is to check first with your doctor. Medical acceptance of the benefits of a well-managed exercise programme is growing, but there are still some doctors who take a negative view of ageing and may be over-cautious. It will help your doctor if you can obtain from the qualified instructor a brief description of what the classes will involve. Activities to avoid are those which involve sudden exertion or strain. Squash, for example, would be an unwise choice for people who aren't fully fit, unlike badminton which is a very good game at almost any level.

Any exercise session should start with a gradual warm-up, and end with a wind-down. All this means is that you begin exercising slowly with some easy swinging or stretching in order to get the circulation going and the oxygenised blood into muscles and joints before performing more vigorous actions. In contrast a wind-down is a gentle relaxing period during which the breathing pattern and heart rate return to normal.

The hazards of inactivity are far more serious than any dangers associated with sensible exercise. But what is sensible? The following Dos and Dont's are suggested by the Sports Council who have been actively campaigning to encourage more older people to participate in physical activities.

- DO have your blood pressure checked if this hasn't been done in the last five years.
- DON'T take vigorous outdoor exercise in either very hot or very cold weather.
- DO play at your own level and avoid the temptation to impress youngsters!
- DON'T carry on exercising if you feel any unpleasant effects, like pain, dizziness or unusual fatigue.

Good all-round exercise

Walking

Some people feel they get sufficient exercise by regular walking. Beware of long winter walks, however, especially if the temperature is low. Breathing deeply in very cold air is not good for you. Medical research has shown that cold temperatures affect the viscosity of the blood.

Walking is a good habit to get into but the same route round the lake in the local park every day can get boring. The leisure departments of some local authorities, particularly those in green belt areas, organise walks through local woodland and countryside, accompanied by a guide who knows the footpaths. There are usually leaflets on display in libraries giving dates and meeting places, along with a rough idea of the distance. This is an ideal way to meet new people in a casual, informal way.

Guided walks are a popular leisure activity in towns, too, particularly those with interesting historical connections. Exploring on foot is often the best way to familiarise yourself with a new place, or to really learn about the nooks and crannies in your own home town. Local tourist guides are often retired people themselves, with a thorough knowledge of local architecture and history. They can point out decorative details on old buildings which you may have passed and missed a hundred times before. For longer walks, check to see if there is a local Ramblers' Association group (see p 71).

As and when you are used to regular walking, you might like to consider the possibility of a walking holiday. The Ramblers' Association have a subsidiary organisation, Ramblers' Holidays, whose brochure offers an impressive range of walking tours, covering five continents. All the tours are carefully graded on a scale which varies from as little as three hours' walking each day to tough mountain walking, using ice picks and crampons! Many tours allow time for sightseeing, visiting archaeological sites, photography and studying wild flowers. Parties are small and many walkers go as singles. If you are interested, write to Ramblers' Holidays, Box 43, Welwyn Garden City, Hertfordshire AL8 6PQ. Tel: 0707 331133.

Cycling

Quicker than walking, more environmentally friendly than bus or car, cycling is also beneficial to health. It reduces blood pressure, improves cardio-vascular fitness, increases stamina and reduces body fat. As a means of transport, a bike is useful for getting about locally and for a leisurely exploration of the wider countryside, combined perhaps with train or car.

Nowadays there's a huge range of different bikes for all purposes, including mountain bikes and folding models which can be stowed in the boot of a car. There's a ready market in second-hand bikes and they're also available for hire.

Safe cycling routes are on the increase in towns and cities and now even include some inter-city routes such as the 70-mile Kennet and Avon towpath linking Bath and Reading. For details of local cycling paths, enquire from your local authority or tourist office.

Membership of the Cyclists' Touring Club (CTC), with a reduced subscription for seniors (over 65), brings touring information for home and abroad, expert advice from their technical department, free third-party insurance and free legal aid in case of accident. Contact the CTC, Cotterell House, 69 Meadrow, Godalming, Surrey GU7 3HS. Tel: 0483 417217. There are over 200 local groups countrywide, many of which organise short trips for beginners.

Swimming

Swimming is one of the best all-purpose forms of exercise. Apart from using many different muscles, it also stimulates the heart and circulation. It is particularly beneficial for people with arthritis because the water supports the body and takes the weight off painful joints.

Many local authority pools run specially designed daytime sessions for retired people at a time when school children aren't splashing about. Many offer lessons for older adult non-swimmers. Some groups of retired people form their own swimming club and book their own pool sessions.

The Settle Water Babies in the Yorkshire Dales had their small beginnings by way of a notice in the local Age Concern shop. Initially, special sessions at the local pool were booked for an experimental six weeks; no one could have anticipated the overwhelming response. Now the Water Babies meet twice a week, subsidised by Age Concern Craven, and as many as 30 people, aged from early 60s to late 80s, regularly attend. Non-swimmers are allocated an experienced swimmer who looks after them on a one-to-one basis, and many have overcome their childhood fear of water and learned to relax and enjoy themselves. The swimmers have even had a go at synchronised swimming, which earned them a lunchtime spot on local television.

If you are already a competent swimmer, you may like to develop the basic skill. You could take a life-saving certificate, perhaps, or offer practical assistance at a swimming session for disabled people. Enquire at your local pool about whether there is such a club or group in your area.

Sport needs you

In the same way as a good swimmer can help less able people, you might find opportunities to put your expertise or sporting skills to good use in the community. As well as coaching, there are vacancies in most sports for referees, linesmen, timers and scorers as well as for keen sports lovers to organise activities for others. This is a wonderful way to naturally keep in touch with the young. The Sports Council, whose address is on page 92, publish a booklet *50-Plus and All to Play For* which outlines a wide range of possibilities.

An up-to-date first aid qualification is always useful. Basic courses are run by local branches of the St John Ambulance Brigade. Up to the age of 65 you can join the St John Ambulance Brigade as a full member and undergo the more intensive training which entitles you to wear their uniform and undertake public duties at sporting and other events. Look in the Yellow Pages for your local branch or, in case of difficulty, contact St John Ambulance Brigade Department, 1 Grosvenor Crescent, London SW1X 7ES.

Try something new

If you've always been active, then keep going. Age itself is no reason for giving anything up. Many competitive sports have special sections for veterans, which takes the pressure off and keeps the game enjoyable. American senior golfer Lee Trevino's comment some years ago that he was tired of playing against the 'flat bellies' and from now on he wanted to play against the 'round bellies' will strike a chord with many older amateur players! Nor is age a good reason for not trying something new in the first place. Many sports and leisure centres now run special sessions for retired people, perhaps one morning or afternoon a week, with an all-in programme including keep fit, table tennis, short mat bowls, etc. The emphasis is on companionship and fun, and beginners are especially welcome.

The idea of these taster sessions is to emphasise the sociability of sport and give you the opportunity to sample what's on offer. The popularity of short mat bowls, for example, is largely due to its sociability. It attracts men as well as women (unlike many keep-fit classes); it requires concentration but isn't over-demanding on energy; and as an indoor activity, it isn't dependent on the kindness of English weather.

Racketball is another easy game, played indoors on a squash court but with a short-handled racquet and a much slower, bouncier ball. It's played by all ages in the United States but is still new in this country where it makes an ideal game for retired people, and uses squash courts which often lie unused in the daytime. Look out for it.

Sometimes, a new sports and leisure centre will organise an open day which gives everyone a chance to look round. If you feel a little shy of going on your own, even to a session for retired people, you could ask a friend to accompany you on a first visit. Alternatively, if you already belong to a club with older members, why not suggest a group visit to the local sports and leisure centre who will probably be only too delighted to welcome you.

How about yoga?

Yoga is an activity for body and mind, and is especially suited to the older age group. There is no reason why someone who has benefitted from a course of gentle keep-fit classes shouldn't be able to cope with a beginners class where you learn stretching, relaxation and breath control. Yoga is non-competitive; you work at your own pace. While it is advisable to attend a class and learn the correct postures, you can also do them on your own at home. There will be plenty of books about yoga in your local library if you wish to find out more. Classes at all levels are advertised locally. The Iyengar Yoga Institute run a class for those with medical conditions, as well as a 59-plus class. The Yoga for Health Foundation run a five-day residential course twice a year for the over-60s. Along with the British Wheel of Yoga, these organisations keep countrywide lists of qualified teachers. Write to them at the following addresses.

The Iyengar Yoga Institute, 223A Randolph Avenue, London W9 1NL. Tel: 071-624 3080.

The Yoga for Health Foundation, Ickwell Bury, Biggleswade, Bedfordshire SG18 9EF. Tel: 0767 27271.

British Wheel of Yoga, 1 Hamilton Place, Boston Road, Sleaford, Lincolnshire NG34 7ES. Tel: 0529 306851.

T'ai-chi Ch'uan

Look out for classes in T'ai-chi, another activity for mind and body. As an exercise routine it is ideal for older people. It is gentle on the body and consists of slow choreographed movements often named after animals and birds, eg the crane spreads out its wing.

The T'ai-chi Ch'uan has been part of Chinese culture for many centuries. You have probably seen documentary film glimpses of elderly Chinese practising the movements in public parks. The movements strengthen muscles, improve breathing and stimulate the circulation. *T'ai-chi* means the Ten Thousand Things, ie everything in the universe; *Ch'uan* means a fisted hand, ie to have yourself within your grasp. As with yoga, it is your choice whether you go on to study the philosophy behind the exercise. Many people are content to practise the beneficial health-giving movements and breathing exercises which help them stay calm in moments of stress. If you have difficulty in finding a class near you, write to the British T'ai-chi Ch'uan Association, 7 Upper Wimpole Street, London W1M 7TD. Tel: 071-935 8444.

Is it accessible?

Many activities are far more widely accessible than they used to be. A lot of the snobbishness associated with certain sports, such as golf and tennis, is disappearing as public facilities improve. Private golf clubs still tend to be expensive and many still cling to outdated attitudes towards women. On a public golf course, however, anyone can hire clubs and buy cheap golf balls. Lessons for beginners or coaching from a professional may be available, and there may even be a practice driving range. Again, if you belong to a social club with retired members, you may be able to arrange a group visit.

Accessibility is easier when you have a car, and widens the choice by enabling you to travel further afield. Another convenience is that you can go ready-dressed in a tracksuit, jogging bottoms or whatever else is appropriate – a useful detail when changing facilities are limited.

Car owners tend to take this freedom and independence for granted. Those who have to rely on public transport are often deterred from leisure pursuits of all kinds because of the difficulties involved, and who can blame them? Going to the swimming baths is not such an attractive proposition if you have to wait twenty minutes at a bus stop before and after. Wouldn't it be nice if car owners would share their transport and offer lifts occasionally?

Holiday sport

Try a new activity

Holidays provide additional opportunities to take part in all kinds of physical activities, often because the facilities are conveniently to hand. Many people who never go near a swimming pool at home enjoy a daily dip in the hotel pool and the occasional game of tennis. Dancing, too, may be an unusual and enjoyable treat for a couple who don't go out much in the evenings. Perhaps when they are back at home, they could look around for afternoon tea dances. Ballroom dancing is a popular activity on special interest holidays. Other holiday activities include bowling and cycling. Look out for special interest holiday brochures in your travel agents, or write to Saga Holidays Ltd (see p 55).

For an opportunity to try out something really different and daring, not just one outdoor activity but many, the YMCA National Centre in the Lake District run Adventure Holidays, including one specially planned for people over 50. Activities on offer include canoeing, orienteering, archery and pony trekking. Details are available from the YMCA Centre, Lakeside, Ulverston, Cumbria LA12 8BD. Tel: 0539 531758.

Outward Bound courses for the over-50s include a centre-based eight-day programme of rock climbing, fell walking, abseiling and orienteering. An expedition course, also for the over-50s, consists of an eight-day cutter sailing course amongst the islands and lochs along the west coast of Scotland. Write for a brochure from Outward Bound, Chestnut Field, Regent Place, Rugby CV21 2PJ. Tel: 0788 560423.

The Youth Hostels Association not only have 250 hostels country-wide, the comfort of which has been greatly improved, but also run a programme of outdoor pursuits geared towards older people who may be unaccustomed to regular exercise. There are also special interest breaks based on activities such as birdwatching and yoga. Enquiries about group holidays for the over-50s should be made to Anne Bower, YHA Development Officer, Westbury, High Street, Napton, Rugby, Warwickshire CV23 8LZ. Tel: 0926 815169.

If you want to track down any of the more unusual sporting activities nearer home, contact your regional Sports Council office or the London office. Nothing is impossible – even windsurfing – but much will depend on your local facilities. *Sport for all*, the annual guide to coaching courses and activity holidays, is available on receipt of a stamped addressed envelope from the Sports Council, 16 Woburn Place, London WC1H 0QP. Tel: 071-388 1277.

The Scottish Sports Council run three national sports centres offering courses for the over-50s including hill walking and ski-ing in the Cairngorms, as well as watersports at the Cumbrae Centre in

Ayrshire. The Council's address is Caledonia House, South Gyle, Edinburgh EH12 9DQ. Tel: 031-317 7200.

Ski-ing

Provided you are generally fit and prepared to put in some prior training, then ski-ing is a perfectly viable option for older holiday-makers, even first-timers. For a sound start, a booklet of exercises called *Ski Legs: Ski-ing for Beginners* is available at a modest price from the Ski Club of Great Britain, 118 Eaton Square, London SW1W 9AF.

Absolute beginners may feel more confident if they join a small party comprising other first-timers. Travel Companions (see p 28), an agency introducing single holidaymakers to fellow travellers, were pleased at the success of their first group ski-ing holidays, arranged at the request of members. At the age of 55, organiser Vera Coppard was a latecomer herself to ski-ing, but four to six weeks beforehand, she began some exercises, and went to dri-ski school.

There are far more artificial ski slopes in Britain than in any other country. The only disadvantage with the dri-ski surface is that you tend to fall a lot harder. Vera stresses that there is more to a ski resort than just the ski-ing and the après-ski entertainment. The mountain scenery is breathtaking – a marvellous opportunity for anyone keen on photography.

Cross-country ski-ing does away with many of the dangers of downhill ski-ing – loss of control and collision. Sometimes called Nordic ski-ing, cross-country ski-ing is featured in most of the ski holiday brochures.

Alan recently took two parties cross-country ski-ing in the Vosges Mountains in France. All the members were over 60, and most of them were beginners. It was specified that everyone should be able to walk ten miles a day; five miles before and after lunch. In Alan's view, walking is an excellent preparation; running is better still. At 63, he enjoys running anyhow, but did a lot more prior to the holiday because he was leading the party. 'You've got to be better than the others. It's a question of safety. Only once did I have to advise everyone to take off their skis and walk down one particular hill because it looked so rocky.'

Cross-country skiers usually follow marked trails. Alan's parties used a route which was really a road, closed to the traffic in winter. The people in the groups were all individual members of the University of the Third Age (see p 52), which has a national Travel Club and which organises trips abroad for its members.

Mind bending

The over-50s comprise the reading, letter-writing, and diary- keeping generation. We may not still do all these pen and paper things but they are part and parcel of our childhood, like parlour games, puzzles and quizzes.

We all enjoy a tussle, getting to grips with a problem, pitting our wits against one another, and not letting something get the better of us. It all helps to keep our minds alert and lively. Many of the following activities are solo pursuits; others need a partner or can be enjoyed as a group effort.

Solo pursuits

CROSSWORDS

Crossword addicts are often convinced that if they complete the crossword in their daily newspaper, it will stop their brains from going rusty. This isn't true! People who do the same newspaper crossword day after day are not as clever as they think. Solving the clues in cryptic crosswords requires lateral thinking but it is possible for the reader to tune into any individual compiler's thought-processes. In time, memory begins to play a bigger part than original thinking. A real mind-stretcher is for the keen crossword solver to change their newspaper fairly frequently. An unfamiliar compiler provides a bigger challenge.

The next stage might be to have a go at compiling crosswords yourself. *The Crossword Dictionary* published by Collins makes useful background reading. Begin by using an existing grid, and existing answers, and try your hand at inventing some fresh clues. Alternatively, you could try a very simple crossword to give to your grandchildren.

For a social occasion, a simple large-print crossword, photocopied many times and tackled in groups at different tables, makes a good icebreaker at a club games session, or even at a party. The first table to provide the correct solution wins a prize. The fact that your crossword is totally original means you can make both answers and clues appropriate to the occasion.

BEAT THE COMPETITION

Competitions are an increasingly popular way of promoting products of all kinds, from cars to cornflakes. Many of us do the occasional competition when it comes our way. We pop the envelope in the letterbox and normally forget all about it. However, there are people whose hobby is 'comping' and who go out of their way to collect competition entry forms. Many of them win dozens of prizes month by month.

The odds on an individual person winning a competition vary enormously; a simple draw will attract far more entries than a competition requiring some degree of skill, which usually means answering one or two questions and writing a slogan. However, there is always the possibility of winning one of the many runner-up prizes. Regular 'compers' take the business of competitions very seriously. They use reference books to supply the answers, and advocate an organised filing system for the entry forms, tokens or labels necessary to enter. Many subscribe to the *Competitor's Companion*, a publication which lists all current and future competitions plus the participating stockists, for it may be important to pick up entry forms quickly while stocks last. Some 'compers' plan their supermarket shopping to cover as many competitions as possible in an individual retail outlet. The magazine also publishes the winning slogans from recent competitions in order to guide and inspire future entrants. The motto here is 'if you don't enter, you won't win'. Send your subscription enquiries to Competitor's Companion, 14 Willow Street, London EC2A 4BH.

JIGSAWS

Jigsaws are a highly enjoyable solo activity but they are not cheap, and compulsive puzzlers can get through bluebell woods and Scottish Highlands at a fast rate!

Anna, a self-confessed jigsaw addict, came up with an ingenious solution to this problem, which others may like to copy. As a regular supporter of her local charity shop, she suggested an arrangement whereby she takes home all the jigsaws donated to the shop each week. She completes them at home and then returns them to the shop, informing the sales assistants which puzzles are complete and can be sold at a higher price, and which have missing pieces.

An alternative is to join the British Jigsaw Library and borrow from the large stock of jigsaws which individual members receive, complete and then return along with their comments. Most members have one to three puzzles at home while others are being swapped. New members can take out a quarterly membership lasting three months which can be converted into annual membership if they wish, though many people choose to be winter-only members. The membership fees do not include postal charges.

The jigsaws themselves are made of wood, and the individually cut pieces are infinitely more satisfying to handle than those made of cardboard. They also fit better and allow for more unusual shapes than factory-produced puzzles. There are no guide pictures supplied; something which does not bother the experienced, and which newcomers seem to get used to. Pictures include landscapes, photographs, famous paintings, etc, and the organiser, Pearl Crompton, will do her best to cater for your preferences. There is a wide variety in style and difficulty. Write to her at the British Jigsaw Library, 8 Heath Terrace, Leamington Spa, Warwickshire CV32 5LY. Tel: 0926 311874.

COMPUTERS

You may already be familiar with computer systems through your work, in which case you will be aware of the variety of functions which are possible with a personal computer (or PC as they are called). Home use in retirement might include:

- keeping club or society membership lists, with addresses and telephone numbers;

- producing address labels for mailing lists;

- producing standard letters with individual variations; very useful if you want to remind certain members that their subscriptions are overdue, or to personalise letters for fundraising;

- producing newsletters, making use of a variety of graphics and type sizes (usually referred to as desktop publishing).

There is a wide range of software available, suitable for playing games such as chess, bridge and backgammon, as well as a huge variety of specially designed computer games.

Computer equipment involves serious money and you need to be sure that what you are buying suits your purposes and that you have the appropriate combination of packages. These are constantly being updated, so beware of stockists, including the multiples, who are trying to shift obsolescent equipment.

A PC is an expensive toy and many owners are unsure how to get the best out of what they've got. Most companies supply a manual, which is fine so long as you are willing to work your way through it and can identify problems as they arise; the accompanying telephone support service is usually for a limited period after purchase. However, there is no shortage of computer magazines on the market, most of which have problem pages or 'clinics', and are highly informative. You can also visit computer exhibitions and attend demonstrations, which usually include question and answer sessions afterwards. Courses are available from a variety of sources (see Chapter 4); for example, the National Extension College (see p 59) offers a basic GCSE course in Computer Studies, which explains the jargon and covers the most popular applications in daily life.

Games for two or more

Games such as whist, bridge, chess, dominoes and Scrabble are often played informally in pubs and clubs. They may also feature in special interest holidays, run by popular hotel chains or travel companies like Saga.

Nearer home, your local library should know of clubs where these games are played regularly, perhaps at a more competitive level.

CHESS

Chess has a much higher profile in Europe that in the UK. Not only is it a more popular game, but the tournaments and championships attract huge numbers of spectators. Yet in spite of the lack of sponsorship in this country, the UK consistently produces top international players.

For information about clubs and tournaments, write to the British Chess Federation, 9a Grand Parade, St Leonards on Sea, East Sussex, TN38 0DD. Tel: 0424 442500.

A variation on the game of chess is correspondence chess, in which each move is recorded on a score sheet and sent by mail to your unseen opponent, either in the UK or abroad. The rules are slightly different in that players are allowed to consult reference books and, with more time for consideration, the game tends to be of a higher standard. Games will obviously last much longer, sometimes up to a year or so, but you are usually playing several games against a number of opponents at the same time.

Chess by post suits people who work unsocial hours; there is a tale of a guard on London Underground who used to work out his moves between stations! However, there is no such person as 'the typical player' – ages range from pre-teens to over 100.

An explanatory booklet, containing information about the many postal chess clubs and tournaments, is obtainable from the British Postal Chess Federation, 173 Gaddesdon Crescent, Waverden Gate, Milton Keynes, MK7 7SF. Tel: 0908 582018.

SCRABBLE

There are over 200 Scrabble clubs in different parts of the country, some meeting during the day, others in the evening. Most of them are friendly, sociable clubs but there are leagues and championships for really competitive players. Theme scrabble is popular; eg around St Valentine's Day, any word associated with love or romance will earn extra points.

Anyone wanting to know if there is a club in their area should send a stamped addressed envelope to the Scrabble Club Coordinator, 42 Elthiron Road, London SW6 4BW. Tel: 071-731 2633. If it turns out that there isn't a club near you, you can ask to be sent the start-a-club pack.

Flora decided to start a Scrabble club in Weston-super-Mare twelve years ago. The national Scrabble Club Coordinator persuaded the local paper to write an article about the project, and it wasn't long before Flora had launched three clubs in the area to cope with the demand.

For the past eight years Flora has been hosting Scrabble holidays run by Saga, together with her husband until his death two years ago. According to Flora, her interest in Scrabble proved to be her salvation at this traumatic time. 'I realised just how many friends I had made through Scrabble and how supportive they all were!'

BRIDGE

Bridge is a more or less social game played with a partner. Good players are always in popular demand for 'making up a four'. Although various social groups run activity sessions entitled 'Bridge for Fun', experienced bridge players will tell you there is nothing funny about playing bridge. Players can get very tight-lipped when partners let them down, and postmortems are commonplace. Beginners may need a thick skin! Opportunities for improving your bridge do exist by way of leisure classes and courses, summer schools, etc. There are also regular bridge columns in newspapers and magazines and the occasional series on television.

For a modest annual fee, you can become a member of the Bridge Union, with its 900 affiliated clubs. Members receive a magazine containing tournament details and information about bridge holidays at home and abroad. For further information, write to the English Bridge Union, Broadfields, Bicester Road, Aylesbury, Bucks HP19 3BG. Tel: 0296 394414.

It's all right to watch TV

You often hear recently retired people expressing the opinion that anyone who is reduced to watching TV during the day must have reached rock bottom. They are not going to let that happen to them, they say, usually with considerable vehemence. Such a conviction is probably indicative of unresolved conflicts; so many people feel guilty about not being gainfully employed. A self-imposed ban on daytime television, based on the assumption that it will rot the brain, simply does not stand up to critical examination.

There is a huge difference between passively watching television and positively watching a selected programme. In fact some of the most interesting programmes are shown in the daytime, in the educational broadcasting slots, and many provide back-up material which you can send for. In addition to these, there are programmes especially compiled for retired people which are shown during the day. These are a useful source of information as well as entertainment. Finally, because many of the more challenging programmes are broadcast late at night, many people prefer to use their video recorder, and watch them next morning when their minds are fresh and clear.

FEEDBACK WANTED

Both television and radio involve two-way communication. Broadcasters badly need feedback from a receptive and interested public, and there are many opportunities for active participation.

First, you can find out how it's done, and be part of an invited studio audience for a specific radio or TV programme. For BBC programmes, write to the Ticket Unit, BBC Radio, Broadcasting House, London

W1A 1AA and the Ticket Unit, BBC Television, Wood Lane, London W12 7SB. For Independent Television programmes, ticket requests should be sent to the regional companies.

Participate actively by responding to national or regional phone-ins, if you feel you can make a relevant contribution based on your experience. Alternatively, you might respond to programmes such as BBC1's 'Bite Back' and 'Points of View' or Channel 4's daily 'Comment' slot. Finally, consider making use of consumer programmes such as BBC1's 'Watchdog', or Radio 4's 'Punters', which are based on listeners' and viewers' own experiences. The relevant addresses are always given at the end of these programmes.

Occasionally, there are open-access programmes like 'Open Door' or Channel 4's 'Free for All', which allow individuals or pressure groups the opportunity to make their own programme with technical advice and support supplied by the television company.

DIY broadcasting

Look out for volunteer opportunities to learn and practise the skills involved in sound broadcasting – programme presenting, researching and producing, recording and editing. All will involve working closely with volunteers of all ages, and training is usually provided. There are a number of possible outlets, and your local library should be aware of groups which are active in your neighbourhood.

COMMUNITY RADIO

Community radio broadcasts a service catering for the needs and interests of a local neighbourhood. Interested groups apply for licences entitling them to restricted air time on specific frequencies. Broadcast material features local people, ethnic music, schools and colleges, clubs and societies. Community radio provides a valuable local service and is non-profitmaking. For more details of the Community Radio movement and of available courses, write to the

Community Radio Association, The Media Centre, 5 Paternoster Row, Sheffield S1 2BX. Tel: 0742 795219.

HOSPITAL RADIO

Hospital radio broadcasts a variety of programmes to patients. Record requests from relatives and friends often form the bulk of the material, although many stations aspire to more ambitious coverage of local events as well as drama. Volunteers take note: many a professional DJ started a flourishing career this way!

TALKING NEWSPAPERS

These are weekly tapes of local news and features which are compiled and distributed to blind and/or housebound people in the area. Advice and assistance in setting up such a scheme is offered by the Talking Newspaper Association of the UK, 90 High Street, Heathfield, East Sussex TN21 8JD. Tel: 04352 6102.

ORAL HISTORY PROJECTS

There is currently an enormous interest in oral history, in which sound recording is used to capture memories of the past. Sensitive listening encourages older people to talk about aspects of their lives and work, in a detail which is rarely documented in written form. Subjects are often regionally based, eg hop-picking in Kent, coal mining in Yorkshire, working in a Lancashire cotton mill, and document our changing culture.

Never think you are too old to learn new tricks like operating a tape recorder. Good editing is dependent on careful listening, which is an art in itself. You will already have many years' experience of serious listening to radio, and will know and recognise the kind of material which makes a good programme.

CHAPTER SEVEN

Home and family

The only gift is a portion of thyself.

RALPH WALDO EMERSON

A recent survey on leisure for the over-50s listed home entertaining, DIY and gardening as the most popular activities. This comes as no surprise since, for many people, home quickly becomes the focus of life when they cease full-time paid employment.

It is very likely that much of the new-found freedom in the initial months of retirement will be spent in making your home more attractive and comfortable, as well as reflecting a new home-based lifestyle. You may wish to convert a spare room into a study to house a word processor; or into a studio where you can spread out your painting or photographic materials; or into a mini-gym. These are all examples of the kind of changes you may wish to make.

However the physical space is rearranged and reorganised, there is still the emotional space to cope with. After many years of co-existence with a growing family, the house may seem abnormally quiet and lacking in soul. Your family may have flown the nest some years ago, but the emptiness may not have been so noticeable while you were still absorbed at work and coming home tired in the evenings.

Now that you're at home for 24 hours a day and meeting fewer people on a daily basis, you run the risk of shrinking horizons. Meeting only the same sort of people as yourself can result in an everyday social life which is insufficiently stimulating. You may wish to meet new people from other backgrounds, and seek the opportunity to make friends out of strangers.

Open house

Are you an easy-going sort of person, prepared to open your home to others outside the normal circle of relatives and friends? If so, there are plenty of opportunities to offer hospitality to appreciative strangers, and to meet people whose lives are different from your own.

There are schemes varying from hosting an occasional Sunday afternoon tea party for housebound people to offering a Christmas visit to an overseas student, or a summer holiday to an inner city child. People who have offered hospitality in these or similar situations invariably stress the two-way benefits derived from a relationship with their guests. It is not unusual for an initial introduction through an organising agency to lead to future visits and, in many instances, lasting friendships.

To tea on Sunday

Contact is a national charity which operates locally. Its branches arrange Sunday tea parties for lonely elderly people living in the neighbourhood, many of whom rarely enjoy an outing of any sort. Tea party hosts and hostesses cater for around a dozen guests on any one occasion. You are not tied to a regular commitment, other than laying on one or two tea parties, probably in the summer when the garden is at its best. A couple of friends or neighbours can perhaps be roped in to help with sandwich-making and washing up. The local branch organiser arranges transport for the guests, from a pool of volunteer car owners, and volunteer escorts assist those with wheel-chairs or walking frames. If this is something which would interest you, write or ring Contact, 15 Henrietta Street, London WC2E 8QH. Tel: 071-240 0630. They will tell you whether there is a branch in your area.

A guest at Christmas

One response to the increasing commercialisation of Christmas is to reaffirm the message of goodwill to all men. This you can do by inviting an overseas student to stay for a weekend. Christmas is a popular time for this and what better reason is there to recreate some of the old Yuletide spirit? Easter is another festive period when overseas students are looking for introductions.

HOST, a national charity founded by the Foreign and Commonwealth Office, the British Council and the Victoria League, aim to introduce overseas students to British life by linking them with UK hosts. Students can be any age from 18 to 58, with or without families of their own. Here's what Mr Wang from China, studying at Imperial College, London, felt about a recent Christmas, which he and his wife spent in Oxford: 'It's a very good experience; we love their family, the pets, the old church, the Christmas gifts in the red "boots" (stockings); the beautiful Oxford city and lots of games – the best experience in the UK.'

As an example of how others see us, the following post-Christmas comment from a student from Zimbabwe is especially revealing: 'To an outsider, the English are like crabs; hard on the outside, but soft on the inside. You have to live with them in order to understand them.'

You can write for a leaflet to HOST, 18 Northumberland Avenue, London WC2N 5BJ. Tel: 071-925 2595.

Offering a refuge

Offers of hospitality are also invited from host families who are willing to give a few days' respite to patients of the Medical Foundation for the Care of Victims of Torture. Many exiles have had to flee from oppressive regimes and now live in London, often in cramped and overcrowded hostels where it is difficult to relax and plan any sort of permanent future. A few days' peace and privacy in a room of their own in an ordinary household can be part of the healing process. 'It made me realise that despite what has happened to me in the past, there are still real human beings in this world,' was how Batool, an Iranian exile, summed up her stay with a Suffolk family.

Host families should ideally live within easy travelling distance of London. Enquiries should be made to Jenny Watson, Medical Foundation for the Care of Victims of Torture, 96 Grafton Road, London NW5 3EJ. Tel: 071-284 4321.

Summer holidays

Each year the Children's Country Holiday Fund (CCHF) arranges for around 3,000 disadvantaged London children to go away on a summer holiday. Some go to camps; others stay with individual households. Your home doesn't have to be literally in the country. Many suburban households offer accommodation and take the children out on day trips.

Prospective hosts will be asked for references and permission for CCHF to follow up positive vetting procedures through Social Services and the police. This is now current practice where the care of children is concerned. More details are available from the Children's Country Holidays Fund, 42/43 Lower Marsh, Tanswell Street, London SE1 7RG. Tel: 071-928 6522.

Sharing your home with animals

Animals have a very positive role to play in helping their owners adjust to retirement. They wake you up in the morning and provide a regular routine in what can be for some an otherwise unstructured day. Dogs need walking, providing you with valuable exercise and social contact; cats remind you when they are hungry, as well as when they want to share affection; even fish respond by rising to the top of the tank at suppertime!

Now that there is more time to spend with your pet, dog owners might consider a dog training club. Ask your vet if there is one near by. Actually, it is the owners who are trained in how to bring up well-behaved, obedient dogs who respond to their commands. No dog is ever too old to learn to get rid of bad habits, so long-term owners as well as first-timers, can benefit from a course, especially now that there are stricter rules concerning pavement and footpath fouling. Dog training clubs also run agility courses; you've probably enjoyed watching the competitions on television.

Till death us do part

It frequently happens that animal lovers who are getting on in years are sometimes reluctant to take on a new pet. The life expectancy for the average cat or dog is around 10 to 15 years. Committing yourself so far ahead may seem like tempting providence.

A natural concern about the consequences, should you die before your pet, needs to be weighed against the positive contribution to your health and well-being that an affectionate animal companion can make, particularly if you live alone. Research has shown that keeping an animal can lower blood pressure and improve recovery from illness. In addition, dogs also offer a degree of protection, while both cats and dogs give enormous pleasure, and certainly ease loneliness at any age. Why not consider 'skipping' the kitten or puppy stage, and instead offer a home to a fully-grown animal, even to one of advancing years (see below)?

Good homes wanted

There is no shortage of pets to choose from in the many rescue shelters run by national charities, and visiting times for the public are usually quite flexible. Home-finding is also carried out by local rescue organisations, who advertise and fundraise on a neighbourhood basis. They may not necessarily have their own boarding premises, but often have an arrangement with a local kennels or cattery. Appointments to see the animals have to be made at a mutually convenient time.

If you don't see a cat or dog which appeals to you on your first visit, then do say so. You will always be welcome to make a return visit. If you have a preference for a particular breed, then let the organisation know, since every effort is made to match dogs and cats with suitable owners. Often though, it is a case of the animal choosing *you*!

Once you have found your future pet, you may not be permitted to take it home with you that day. Home-vetting procedures vary among rescue organisations, but they often include an inspection of the prospective home. This is a necessary precaution for animals which have often already known both cruelty and neglect. The fact that you are retired and at home all day will be strong factors in your favour.

For cat lovers, a free leaflet listing cat rescue organisations is obtainable by sending a stamped addressed envelope to Adopt-a-Cat, PO Box 1112, Shoreham-by-Sea, West Sussex BN43 6SD. Dog lovers might consider a greyhound, a working dog with a very early retirement age. A racing greyhound's professional life is over at the age of three or four – the equivalent of a 20-year-old in human terms! These dogs are fit and healthy, docile and affectionate and settle down happily into domestic life. They do not need as much exercise as you might think; two half-hour walks each day at a good pace is sufficient, although more is welcome. An excellent leaflet giving practical advice on diet and training is available from the Retired Greyhound Trust, 24/28 Oval Road, London NW1 7DA. Tel: 071-267 9256. There is a strict vetting procedure involved, and this takes time. In fact, people who have been greyhound owners in the past could help speed up the home-finding process by offering themselves as members of a countrywide team of volunteer visitors, checking out the homes of prospective owners.

Visiting with your dog

A responsible owner of a friendly, sociable dog might be interested in joining a countrywide visiting scheme run by PRO-Dogs. The scheme is known as PAT, and stands for PRO-Dogs Active Therapy. Its organisers believe in the therapy that affectionate dogs can provide, and they arrange for selected dog owners to visit hospital wards and residential homes, where life for the patients may sometimes be unstimulating and remote. The opportunity to pat and stroke a responsive dog has been proved to be beneficial for a variety of patients, young and old. For some, it is a rare contact with the outside world.

Interested owners must first become full members of PRO-Dogs, since this covers them for insurance purposes. Dogs must also be registered and independently checked for temperament. Once accepted for the scheme, your dog wears a specially engraved PAT disc on its collar. Some hospitals and establishments have arrangements for paying a visitor's travel expenses but this needs to be agreed prior to the visit. To find out more about the scheme, write to Pets as Therapy, PAT Dog Scheme, Rocky Bank, 4 New Road, Ditton, Kent ME20 6AD. Tel: 0732 848499.

Another scheme involving animals and people is the People-Pet Partnership. It arranges for responsible dog owners to visit schools, Brownie/Cub packs, etc with their pet, and to give a talk on animal care. Such visits encourage children to develop responsible attitudes to pet ownership. Teaching materials are provided and are aimed at different age groups. The People-Pet Partnership started in the United States, but is a relatively new organisation here. However, it is expanding, and new groups are being set up in different parts of the country. Many of the members belong to dog training clubs. To find out whether there is a group in your area, contact Christine Walker, 30 Shedbury Lane, Basingbourn, Royston, Herts SG8 5PH. Tel: 0763 244437.

Welfare schemes

Older people who are concerned about the responsibility of caring for a pet may be reassured by joining a welfare scheme. These are schemes to look after pets in cases of accident, emergency or death of the owner. Several animal charities run such schemes. They all stress the importance of making a Will which includes instructions regarding the future welfare of your pet. The charities are happy to advise on the correct wording.

The National Canine Defence League (NCDL) supply a Canine Care Card which you keep with you, rather like an organ donor card. In case of accident or death, it provides an indication of your dog's whereabouts, and the name, address and telephone number of the person who has agreed to look after it. The card also refers to the whereabouts of your Will, since your executor needs to have the address of NCDL kennels if you wish your dog to be taken there. Wherever possible, NCDL will try and find a suitable new home for your dog. Otherwise, they will look after it. A leaflet is available from the National Canine Defence League, 1 Pratt Mews, London NW1 0AD. Tel: 071-388 0137.

The Animal Welfare Trust has two emergency schemes. Pet Concern, applicable to senior citizens and disabled people only, may provide some financial help with short-term board while an animal's owner is in hospital or convalescing. This temporary care may be at one of the Trust's centres, or in a private kennel or cattery. Applications are usually made via social workers or GPs.

In contrast to this, the Members Emergency Pet Care Scheme is available to all on membership of the Trust. Again, short-term emergency care is available. Leaflets are available from the Animal Welfare Trust, Tyler's Way, Watford By-pass, Watford, Herts WD2 8HQ. Tel: 081-950 8215.

The Cinnamon Trust was set up especially to assist older pet owners by providing sanctuaries for pets whose owners are ill or have died. Based in Cornwall, the Trust aims to open a wider network of sanctuaries as and when funds permit. Meanwhile their countrywide pet-help scheme uses volunteers to act as dog walkers for invalids, or to provide pet foster care in case of illness. The Cinnamon Trust is at Poldarves Farm, Tresowe Common, Germoe, Penzance, Cornwall TR20 9RX. Tel: 0736 850291.

Pet fostering

If you have some experience of animals but don't want the all-year-round commitment of pet ownership yourself, you might enjoy looking after an animal on an occasional basis. There is also the bonus of knowing you are setting the pet owner's mind at rest, be they on holiday or in hospital. In addition to the volunteers recruited countrywide by the Cinnamon Trust (see above), your local vet may be able to introduce you to owners in need of a dog-minding or walking service, on either a voluntary or a paid basis.

There are also commercial agencies such as Home and Pet Care, Home Sitters and Universal Aunts, who advertise for mature animal lovers to supply a live-in service for clients away on holiday or business. For someone with the additional experience of keeping livestock or horses, this could be an ideal working holiday. Needless to say, good references are required. You can contact these agencies at the following addresses.

Home and Pet Care Ltd, PO Box 19, Penrith, Cumbria CA11 7AA. Tel: 06998 515.

Home Sitters, Buckland Wharf, Buckland, Aylesbury, Bucks HP22 5LQ. Tel: 0296 630730.

Universal Aunts Ltd, 19 The Chase, London SW4 0NP. Tel: 071-738 8937.

One of the most rewarding pet care tasks is to be involved in the early stages of training a working dog, whose life will be useful and highly valued. Hearing Dogs for the Deaf is an organisation which trains dogs to act as the ears of deaf people. A hearing dog is taught to respond to familiar household sounds – the doorbell, telephone, oven timer or baby – and to make physical contact with the owner, leading them to the source of the sound. The dogs also provide deaf people with confidence and companionship, particularly if they live alone.

Potential hearing dogs come largely from rescue centres. They are selected for their intelligence and alertness as well as for their steady temperament. Before intensive training at a centre in Oxford, and before being matched with a future deaf owner, a trainee dog spends up to six months with volunteer foster parents or 'socialisers'. Socialisers are asked to take the dog out with them in their car, to travel with it on public transport, and generally to meet a wide range of people, including young children. A socialiser can live anywhere in the country but must attend the monthly obedience classes at the Oxford Training Centre. Petrol is reimbursed and a reasonable sum contributed towards feeding costs. For further details, write to Hearing Dogs for the Deaf, The Training Centre, London Road (A40), Lewknor, Oxon OX9 5RY. Tel: 0844 353898.

A similar scheme involving puppy walkers is run by the National Guide Dogs for the Blind who have seven regional training centres. You can contact them at Hillfields, Burghfield Common, Reading RG7 3YG. Tel: 0734 835555.

Family life

When people bemoan the so-called breakdown of family life, they tend to forget that the tight family circle of yesteryear often cruelly excluded members who didn't conform. The person who married someone from another race or religion, or who gave birth to a child outside marriage, or who had any kind of mental or emotional illness was ostracised and forgotten. Society is generally more tolerant today; the rigid family circle has taken on a more flexible form, changing its shape in response to divorce and re-marriage, as well as expanding to include a fourth generation of great-grandparents, an additional layer which is quite common today. Many families also include 'fringe' members who are linked by co-habitation rather than marriage. What matters in such cases is the quality of relationships, not how they are legally defined.

A flourishing family tree is an umbrella under which individual households, single and multiple, and including as many as four generations, are linked to each other.

Being a grandparent

Grandparenting has always been one of the most significant and deeply-felt of all family roles. It often brings with it a strengthening of family ties, and the promise of a new lease of life with interests and activities to be shared. Although in theory grandparents can be any age from about the mid-30s onwards, it may not be until you are free from the time-consuming demands of a job that you have the time to make an effort as a grandparent.

Babysitting and childminding may be enjoyable tasks, but they are largely supportive of the parental role. Now you're retired, your involvement can be more individual and constructive. Exploring the world through the eyes of an older child, by going on shared holidays, trips and outings, is a rewarding two-way experience. This isn't exclusive to grandparents, of course; it's often enjoyed by older aunts and uncles, too.

E

Make it positive

Positive grandparenting means not trying to live up to some sentimental stereotype. Why are grandparents invariably described as 'doting'? Most adults have an age group they prefer when it comes to children, so if you don't dote on babies, don't feel the need to pretend. Try to shrug off society's stereotype of grandparents, whether it's knitting cardigans, buying pretty dresses, imparting wisdom to the young or taking your grandchild fishing. Neither should you allow yourself to be manipulated by your grown-up children into fulfilling whatever grandparent role they feel is appropriate (or useful!) Never feel pressurised to compete with the other set of grandparents, especially over present buying. There's more to being a grandparent than trying to be Santa Claus, the Easter Bunny and Mary Poppins.

Establish your own identity as a grandparent, developing the kind of relationship which you are happy and confident to sustain. The hard part is often the balancing act required between relating to each of your grandchildren individually, and not appearing to have favourites. This is not always easy, particularly if one child or one set of grandchildren is noticeably better behaved than another. Alternatively, one family may live much further away and the fact that you see much less of them may cause conflicts for everyone. Letters and phonecalls to the grandchildren (as well as to your children) can help a lot here, as well as visits. Try and encourage an equal, two-way relationship. Don't always expect the others to be the ones to write, visit or phone. An unexpected and supportive phonecall can mean such a lot to a hard-pressed son or daughter!

Having grandchildren to stay with you for a few days in the school holidays helps them establish an independent identity and consolidates your individual relationship with them. They may prefer to come with brothers, sisters or cousins, or take turns to come on their own. You can then enjoy the caring role without too much parental intervention. It may be unfair but there's nothing a child enjoys more than hearing conspiratorial stories of what their parents got up to when they were young!

Occasional three-generational holidays on neutral ground are a good way to experience closeness without emotional claustrophobia. The venue may be a self-catering holiday cottage or villa, either in the UK or abroad, or even a residential activity holiday which keeps everyone busy (see p 91).

When to say no

Being retired and at home in the daytime can be a mixed blessing in some families. Sons and daughters living near by may take it for granted that your free time is at their disposal for routine domestic tasks such as babysitting, gardening or decorating.

Maternal grandmothers are the most common carers of young children whose mothers work full-time. This may be a convenient arrangement, but family duty taken to extremes can have its price. Many women seek emotional fulfilment entirely through their family, often at the expense of making independent friendships with people of their own age group. This can have serious consequences in later life.

Family support is too often based on assumptions rather than freely discussed and mutually agreed arrangements. Obviously, emergencies will arise and only you can decide on your own priorities. Help out, by all means, but don't let your contribution be taken for granted. It does no harm to let it be known that minding the children in the school holidays will mean you missing out on your favourite pastimes. Think of New Year's Eve. Too many grandparents are regarded as routine babysitters. Mightn't they want to go to the ball?

Many grown-up children, of course, are sensitive to their parents' rights to an independent life, and are grateful for each and every offer of help. It's all a question of balance. Similarly, most grandparents understand that all positive opportunities for inter-generational contact are important and should be welcomed. After all, grandparenting can't be taken for granted.

Grandparenting at risk

Research conducted by Age Concern England, who celebrate an annual Grandparents Day, shows that while grandparents may play an important role in the lives of young children, there is strong evidence that their contact lessens with the passing years.

Social changes which account for the loss of contact with grandchildren include two important factors. The increasing mobility demanded by jobs these days often causes families to live at greater distances apart, even overseas, perhaps, where regular visiting isn't possible. In addition to this, one in every three marriages is ending in divorce. This often results in paternal grandparents losing touch with their grandchildren, especially with those who are too young to have formed a relationship independent of their parents.

Other social shifts have produced an increasing number of would-be grandparents, who 'live in hope'. Grandparents-in-waiting may include any of the following: parents of daughters who have opted to remain single, perhaps preferring the satisfaction of an interesting career to marriage; parents of a couple who choose to be childless; parents of professional couples who postpone pregnancy until later in life.

The regret and longing of a would-be grandparent in any of these situations is undeniable, but it shouldn't get in the way of family relationships. Other people's personal decisions, temporary or permanent, have to be respected and accepted. However, if any of these situations apply to you, and you are fond of the company of young children, it may be possible to find alternative outlets.

Substitutes for grandparenting

Precious as grandchildren are, contact with the young is not necessarily dependent on blood ties. Never have children been in greater need of adults who take a personal interest in their well-being. Never have the older generation been so removed from daily contact with children and teenagers.

In the same way that childless couples can satisfy their parental aspirations through adoption or fostering, would-be grandparents (be they married or single) will find many ways of keeping in touch with young children once they start looking. It could be an informal friendship with a neighbour's family, initiated by an offer of babysitting and building from there. It might take the form of a volunteer job, such as helping at a clinic to weigh babies, or assisting at a playgroup. Many primary schools now welcome the help of outsiders in the classroom, whether they are parents or unrelated volunteers.

Volunteer Reading Help is a national scheme through which interested volunteers help children to learn to read. A recent government development grant has enabled the scheme to expand its network of regional branches. Volunteers do not need formal qualifications. What is required is an enthusiasm for children, books and language, as well as common sense and patience. Volunteers receive a training, not in reading methodology, but in order to provide them with confidence. Reading support for children is provided in a relaxed atmosphere through play, word games, puzzles and rhymes, all of which help them recognise letter shapes, improve their memory and practise their reading skills. To find out whether there is a scheme in your area, contact Volunteer Reading Help at Unit 111, The Foundry, Blackfriars Road, London SE1 8EN. Tel: 071-721 7156.

Keeping in touch

Whether you're a natural or a surrogate grandparent, you'll want to keep in touch with the world of the young, and discover how things have changed since you were a parent. However sceptical you may be of current thinking on child care and education, the least you can do is ensure your views are based on up-to-date information rather than fossilised ideas.

BIRTH/BABYHOOD

The National Childbirth Trust are planning to publish a leaflet which has been specially written for grandparents, acquainting them with current antenatal procedures and birth arrangements. Enquiries should be sent to the National Childbirth Trust, Alexandra House, Oldham Terrace, Acton, London W3 6NH. Tel: 081-992 8637.

TODDLERS AND PRE-SCHOOL

A good way of getting back in touch is to browse through the current magazines on children and parenthood. One of the best is a monthly issue called *Under Five*, produced for the Pre-school Playgroups Association. It is on sale in newsagents but, in case of difficulty, write to Under Five Subscriptions, Hainault Road, Little Heath, Romford, Essex RM6 5NP. Tel: 081-597 7335.

The Pre-school Playgroups Association run a variety of courses, recognised countrywide, for playgroup assistants and leaders. Interested individuals might seek out the useful publication entitled *What Children Learn in Playgroup*. Details can be obtained from the Pre-school Playgroup Association, 61–63 Kings Cross Road, London WC1X 9LL. Tel: 071-833 0991.

SCHOOL-AGE CHILDREN

The Advisory Centre for Education (ACE) offer independent guidance on the workings of the state school system. Handbooks and information sheets are published on many topics including the role of the school manager or governor.

For a list of publications, contact the Advisory Centre for Education, Unit 1B, Aberdeen Studios, 22–24 Highbury Grove, London N5 2EA. In addition, a telephone advice line operates in the afternoons, Monday to Friday, on 071-354 8321.

Tracing your family

Tracing one's family history seems to be a growing interest. Maybe this is the result of a general insecurity and unrest in the world today, or perhaps it is a basic human need. Whatever the reason, it seems to hold a particular fascination for older people. Researching your family can help to put your own life in perspective, and may encourage you to come to terms with your own mortality. It is certainly a time-consuming hobby and one that is ideally suited to the retirement years.

Into the past

Tracing your ancestors through earlier generations is a popular subject for leisure classes and courses. These are fine as an introduction and as a means to get you started; however, most of the research will eventually have to be done alone, in your own time.

Joining a family history society will support you in your search; other members will be there to offer advice when you get stuck. A countrywide list of such societies and a useful publications list may be obtained by sending a large stamped addressed envelope to Pauline Saul, Administrator, Federation of Family History Societies, 5 Mornington Close, Copthorne, Shrewsbury SY3 8XN. Also available from the Federation is the leaflet *Tracing your Ancestors*, written in conjunction with the Society of Genealogists and the British Tourist Authority. (The BTA's involvement reflects the number of visitors from abroad who come to the UK each year in search of their roots.)

Your first step into the past should be talking to your oldest surviving family members. They may also be able to identify faces in old photographs. (For the benefit of future family historians, you could now make a point of captioning all family photographs, not only putting names to faces, but also stating the place, date and occasion.)

A key date for those interested in tracing their family history is 1837, which in England saw the start of the centralised system of recording all births, marriages and deaths. There is an index to this at St Catherine's House in the Aldwych, London. Prior to 1837 you are dependent on parish records, which may involve your visiting the actual parish. Procedures vary in Scotland, Northern Ireland, the Isle of Man and the Channel Islands.

Other records commonly consulted by genealogists are census returns, Wills and Chancery Court proceedings, all of which are to be found in the Public Records Office, whose buildings are in Chancery Lane, London and at Kew. You need to make an advance application for a Reader's ticket. It is interesting to note that the Home Office records for convicts deported to Australia are relatively complete, and it is even possible to trace the court which passed the original sentence. Ironically, emigrants who travelled of their own free will are not so well documented or easily traced!

For those who live within easy reach of London, the use of the library at the Society of Genealogists may save longer journeys. This library contains the largest collection of copies of parish records in the country. There are also Army and Navy lists, clergy and medical directories, and rare items such as an index of apprentices (1710–74). There are fees for the use of the library by non-members. For full details, send a stamped addressed envelope to the Society of Genealogists, 14 Charterhouse Buildings, Goswell Road, London EC1M 7BA. Tel: 071-251 8799.

In the present

Instead of digging about in the past in search of your family roots, you may prefer the idea of tracing relatives with whom you have lost touch. A forthcoming occasion such as the 90th birthday of a relative may inspire you to arrange a reunion of long-lost cousins and other kith and kin who you haven't seen or heard from in years. In this situation, you would probably be linking rather than tracing. How far you take the search is up to you and depends on what you want to achieve – a relatively simple, extended family party or a gathering of the clans.

Some people take the process a stage further, tracing people who bear the same surname, particularly if it is an unusual one. Many of these 'one-name' groups form their own organisation and circulate a newsletter. A logical consequence is a gathering of the clan, a momentous task which can take up to two years to arrange. A booklet from the Federation of Family History Societies (see p 119) *Organising a One-Name Society Gathering* gives advice on how to set about this.

Adoption

Sometimes there are sensitive and personal reasons why one person wishes to trace another. In the past, adoption was shrouded in secrecy. It is now generally recognised that individuals have a basic right to know their origins. The right of adults who were adopted as babies or children to have full information about their birth parent and access to their birth records was enshrined in the 1976 Adoption Act. Birth mothers, however, have had no similar right of access to trace their lost children until now.

Some older women who had their babies adopted may prefer to leave painful memories to the past. Recent research from Barnados reveals that 40 or 50 years ago most birth mothers felt they had no choice but to part with their babies; the social pressures for unmarried mothers in those days were too great. However, many mothers have never forgotten their babies and often express a wish to be traced.

The Adoption Contact Register, set up in May 1991, provides contact, so long as this is by mutual desire. A leaflet entitled *The Adoption Contact Register: Information for Adopted People and their Relatives* is available free of charge from the General Register Office, Adoptions Section, Smedley Hydro, Trafalgar Road, Birkdale, Southport PR8 2HH.

Counselling and information on all aspects of adoption is available from the Post Adoption Centre, 8 Torriano Mews, Torriano Avenue, London NW6 2RZ. Tel: 071-284 0555. Another agency which can advise on search and also act as an intermediary is the National Organisation for the Counselling of Adoptees and Parents (NORCAP), 3 New High Street, Headington, Oxford OX3 7AJ. Tel: 0865 750554.

Much of the emphasis placed on counselling is in order to save the disappointment caused by false expectations. Yesterday's baby is today's stranger. A good outcome may not necessarily be a happy one, say Barnados. Their research on reunions discovered the following: first meetings are emotional and stressful; contact tends to decrease after the first few meetings; and social differences arising from different upbringings can interfere with the relationship. Most people, however, feel no regrets about a reunion and say that they feel more complete and fulfilled as a result. However painful, it is a positive experience which leaves you better able to get on with your life.

GETTING BACK IN TOUCH

Most people, however rich their social lives, can think of long lost friends they would like to meet up with again. These may be old class-mates from your schooldays or an interesting acquaintance met on holiday whose phone number you have mislaid. So where do you start?

A useful free guide from BT, *The phone detective's guide to getting back in touch*, is written in association with Pinkerton's Security Services and tells you how to go about tracking down someone from your past. Ring the BT Freephone number 0800 800 864 for a copy.

CHAPTER EIGHT

You only live once

Too much of a good thing can be wonderful.

MAE WEST

Most of us indulge in the occasional daydream. It's often about some unusual or daring thing we'd like to do one day, as and when we have the time. It may be no more than a vague inclination, filed away indefinitely at the back of the mind, with no need of any positive action on our part.

Why shouldn't we turn wishful thinking into reality? The third age is increasingly concerned with exploration and putting ideas into action. Next time you find yourself reading an article or watching something on TV and responding along the lines of 'Mmm, I'd quite like to do that one day', follow it up and do something about it straight away before the momentum is lost. The result may be some mad moments or a day to remember. You won't know until you try.

New experiences

Up, up and away

A trip in a hot air balloon is a memorable experience. Imagine drifting in an open wicker basket high above a panorama of green and yellow patchwork fields. 'Like nothing else I've ever known'; 'It's unbelievably quiet and peaceful up there'; and 'It's almost spiritual' are all typical descriptions of this aerial adventure.

Balloon trips are becoming a popular birthday or anniversary treat, costing around £120 per person with discounts available for groups. Balloons do not fly from airfields but from grassy sheltered sites. As flights are dependent on light wind with no rain or turbulence, ideal conditions are most likely to be in the early morning and late afternoon and evening.

While the pilot has a good deal of control over the rising and sinking of the balloon, the steering will largely depend on the wind, which may blow in different directions at different heights. Flights last around one hour and the landing point is seldom in the same place as the launch; a retrieve vehicle on the ground follows the balloon's course and returns the passengers to the take-off site.

A company called Ballooning World, a certified Civil Aviation Authority Air Operator, organise flights from a number of sites in the UK. Their brochure is available from Ballooning World, 18/19 Linhope Street, London NW1 6HT. Tel: 071-706 1021. Sometimes flights have to be cancelled due to weather conditions, in which case another booking is offered at a mutually convenient time.

Historical re-creation

As we grow older and are nearer to taking our own place in history, the past becomes more relevant. There are a number of exciting ways in which you can develop an interest in the past.

Most people have a favourite period in English history, which explains the popularity of historical re-enactment societies. Their events are always worth looking out for.

The Sealed Knot, whose name is taken from the small band of Royalists who planned the restoration of Charles II, is the biggest military enactment organisation in Europe and has over 5,000 members. Other groups include the English Civil War Society, the Richard III Society and, more recently formed, the Napoleonic Society and the Victorian Military Society. As well as battle recreations, these organisations also arrange living history events and exhibitions. Your local library should have their details.

Kentwell Hall is an Elizabethan manor house in Suffolk which is currently being restored. Each year an event takes place for three weeks in June and July, which aims to re-create a distinct aspect of Tudor England. Recent re-creations have included Kentwell 1588, the Great Armada; Kentwell 1605, the Gunpowder Plot, and Kentwell 1553, the short reign of Queen Jane, Lady Jane Grey.

The annual event is organised by the owners, Patrick and Judith Phillips, together with a small band of helpers. Parts of the house are appropriately furnished, and the gardens and farm are arranged as they would have appeared at the specified date. Around 500 participants are selected to portray the inhabitants of the manor, from the grandest gentry to the most menial serfs. Activities include making beeswax and tallow candles, tapestry or broderie, archery and brewing. There are also minstrels, musicians, dancers and children playing games. There are briefing sessions beforehand, and participants are expected to do their own background reading and provide their own costumes, including shoes.

The object of the re-creation project is to promote history education, to show off a historic house, to raise funds for the restoration programme and to provide a stimulating and enjoyable experience for everyone. Participants can stay for one, two or three weeks. Meals are provided, and there is free camping space near by for those who bring their own tent. Otherwise there is local bed and breakfast accommodation which you book and pay for yourself. If you would be interested in taking part in this unique experience, write to Kentwell Hall, Long Melford, Suffolk CO10 9BA. Tel: 0787 310207.

Digging up the past

For those who are interested in history but prefer to keep fact and fiction in separate compartments, an alternative 'unique experience' might be an archaeological excavation.

Excavations take place on UK sites from March to September and extra help is often needed. Volunteers don't have to be experienced, but should be fit enough to cope with bending and stooping. Additional skills such as photography or the ability to draw can come in useful for processing finds, all of which have to be carefully washed and recorded.

To find out whether there are digs in your area which need volunteers, contact your County Archaeologist. Alternatively, on receipt of a stamped addressed envelope, the Council for British Archaeology will send you the address of the regional group secretary in your area. Digs are also listed in a publication entitled *British Archaeological News*, copies of which are available for consultation in major reference libraries. It is also available on subscription from the

Council for British Archaeology, 112 Kennington Road, London SE11 6RE. Tel: 071-582 0494.

A glimpse into the future

See for yourself how the world may run in the future at the Centre for Alternative Technology at Machynlleth, near the coast in mid-Wales. As well as viewing the working displays of wind, solar and water power, visitors can inspect an energy-efficient house.

Residential courses lasting two to five days are held throughout the year devoted to renewable energy systems, organic gardening and woodland management. In addition, volunteers are welcome to work at the Centre for a week or fortnight, and to help staff manage the project. The accommodation, surrounded by mountain scenery, is simple, but there are a few single rooms. For more information, write to the Centre for Alternative Technology, Machynlleth, Powys, Wales SY20 9AZ. Tel: 0654 702400.

Fantasy roles

We all need the opportunity to live out our fantasies and indulge in some harmless role-play from time to time. Provided our feet are on the ground most of the time, a little experimentation and escapism now and then will not come amiss. Here are some safe suggestions for would-be world champions who might choose to tear round the racing circuit, or for potential antiques experts to indulge in a little buying and selling on the side.

Demon drivers

It's perfectly possible to experience the thrills of dangerous driving in a safety-conscious environment under expert guidance. For driving courses with a difference, including go-karting, four-wheel drive and rallying, write for the list produced by the English Tourist Board, Thames Tower, Black's Road, London W6 9EL, remembering to enclose a stamped addressed envelope. A couple of examples from Brands Hatch are detailed below. Both offer motorists the opportunity to test their skills and try out new challenges.

SKIDMASTER

Driving a car which suddenly goes into an uncontrollable spin is a terrifying experience. Would you know how to handle it? You can learn emergency car control techniques by way of one-to-one instruction in a Skidmaster car. Simulated skids start at 5 mph, so that you can progressively develop your skills. This course was previously only available to professional drivers, such as the police. Now you can have a go too.

FOUR-WHEEL DRIVE AND OFF-ROAD SCHOOL

Also run by Brands Hatch, this has been described as the nearest any motorist can get to a commando course. Here's your chance to drive a Suzuki Samurai across terrain which is impassable on foot.

On the initial one-hour course, an instructor provides a full briefing and expert guidance as you tackle treacherous obstacles, such as two water splashes, a log balance, and ditches wide enough to swallow the vehicle. A winding route give friends and family the chance to photograph you in action at the wheel. The two-hour super course goes on to include tuition on the 'axle twist', before finishing with the thickly-wooded Jungle run.

For more information about Skidmaster and the Four-Wheel and Off-Road School, write to Brands Hatch, FREEPOST, Fawkham, Dartford, Kent DA3 8NG. Tel: 0474 872367.

Treasure seekers

There's something of the dealer in all of us. Anyone who has ever helped out at a jumble sale or browsed in a charity shop will be familiar with the magnetic attraction of finding a bargain. After all, one person's rubbish is another's precious find.

CAR BOOT SALES

The simplest form of trading available to everyone is the car boot sale, which offers the opportunity to clear out domestic clutter, make some money and have a good day out. All you need is a mixed collection of things to sell – and transport.

Many so-called boot sales are held indoors, in premises such as church and school halls. They are advertised locally, and a contact telephone number for the organiser is provided. Ask whether there is a discount for an advance booking, whether tables are provided and, if so, how big are they?

Before participating in a car boot sale, it's a good idea to go along to one or two first to see the kinds of things people are selling and the prices they are asking. You will also be able to judge how popular that particular venue is with customers, and how good the facilities are, eg tea and coffee, toilets and parking.

Anything goes at a car boot sale – that is their appeal. Typical items might be kitchen utensils, children's toys and games, vases and bric-a-brac, paperbacks, household items like towels or table cloths, and junk jewellery – in other words anything you no longer have a use for. Remember, people are looking for bargains, so pile your goods high and sell them cheap. Be prepared for those customers who don't feel they're getting value for money if they don't haggle.

You will need the following items with you on the day.

- A large cloth to drape over the table. An old velvet curtain makes an attractive background for the worst collection of jumble.
- Felt-tip pens and peel-off labels for pricing (and re-pricing).
- A pair of scissors, string, and sellotape.
- Spare plastic carrier bags are useful for customers.
- A lot of loose change for all those five-pound notes.
- An apron with a 'kangaroo pouch' in which to put the money, or a jam jar, or a locking cash box.

- Plastic ice cream cartons are useful for keeping small items together like buttons, beads, brooches, electric plugs, etc.
- Wear low-heeled, comfortable shoes and take along a folding stool. You're going to be there for a few hours.

COLLECTABLES

When you get round to sorting out the loft, you may come across bits and pieces which are worth quite a lot today as collectables; things like old 'Dinky' cars, toy soldiers, Meccano, flying ducks, comics like the *Beano* and *Dandy*, school stories by Angela Brazil, schoolboy and schoolgirl annuals, old football programmes, postcards, etc.

The golden rule is not to part with anything until you've done your homework and checked on its value. You may well be surprised. Look round local fairs and antiques markets to see if there are similar items and what the prices are like. You could also look in any books you can find in the library or in bookshops. There is a *Which? Guide to Buying Collectables*, published by Hodder & Stoughton. Also, keep your eyes open for newspaper articles, especially in the weekend editions of the serious newspapers which often have articles on popular collectables.

If you think you have found something of worth which you want to sell, take the object or a colour photograph of it to a reputable sale-room and ask for a valuation. They may suggest selling in a specialised sale which will probably fetch a higher price, although there may be some delay. The auctioneers take a commission on the sale, so it's in their interest to get the best possible price.

Always seek a second opinion, and don't ever part with anything to anyone at the door. Reputable dealers don't work that way. Of course, you might decide that you'd quite like to start collecting yourself as a hobby, using the couple of items you already have as the basis of a collection. Alternatively, you may prefer to sell your bits and pieces, and start afresh with something which appeals to you more.

Whatever your favoured collectable, whether it is buttons, crested china, or garden gnomes, the advice is the same.

- Find out as much as you possibly can by background reading.
- Cut out and keep a file of newspaper and magazine articles.
- Train your eye by seeing and comparing; visit fairs, flea markets, secondhand shops and museums.
- Invest in a good magnifying glass.

An interesting, inexpensive series of publications is the *Album* series from Shire Publications. These little books are small enough to slip into your pocket, and individual titles cover a huge range of collectables including *Toy Soldiers*; *Teddy Bears and Soft Toys*; *Thimbles*; *Playing Cards and Tarots*; *Constructional Toys*; *Old Sewing Machines*, and literally dozens of other specialities. They are on sale at good bookshops but, in case of difficulty, you can contact the publisher direct at Cromwell House, Church Street, Princes Risborough, Aylesbury, Bucks HP27 9AZ. Tel: 08444 4301.

Once you've become an expert in your field, you'll be able to browse round at car boot sales, street markets and second-hand shops with added zest. Who knows what treasures you'll find?

ATTENDING AN AUCTION

Bargain hunting for bric-a-brac at fairs and flea markets is one thing; attending an auction for something bigger and more expensive is another. Many people would like to buy interesting pieces of furniture this way, but there is a widespread popular fear that if you accidentally twitch an eyebrow at the wrong time, you may get landed with a highly expensive antique. This only happens in film comedies. The truth is that it can be difficult to attract the auctioneer's attention when you genuinely want to bid, particularly if there are well-known dealers at the sale. An alternative to bidding yourself is to leave a written bid; there are often bidders' forms which you fill in beforehand. Alternatively, you can ask a porter to bid on your behalf, which should be worth a tip if you are successful.

There is usually a viewing day before a sale. Once you've seen something appealing, set yourself a price limit and don't exceed it. If you do not wish to pay cash, check in advance that the auction room will accept your cheque. You will also need transport, or there may be a storage charge. Some firms will deliver, but check their charges first.

The atmosphere of salerooms can be addictive, and you can have some interesting days out, whether or not you decide to buy. A highly recommended book is *Town and Country Auctions in Britain: the Bargain Hunter's Handbook*, published by the AA. This lists auctions and viewing times, and contains many nuggets of interesting information.

Postscript: it's your retirement

You may find it useful to monitor your progress in the early stages of your retirement, because those 50 full and shining hours can so easily disappear without a trace. A weekly diary is one way of keeping track of your time. You can then look back at, say, six-monthly intervals to see how you feel about your lifestyle and the way things are developing. It may take a couple of years to achieve a balanced mix of activities. Not every avenue you explore will be the right one for you, but false starts are soon forgotten as you make new contacts.

Always keep some space in your week for any new opportunities which come your way. 'If you want something done, ask a busy person' is a well-worn cliché, but is particularly true in retirement when people seem to divide into two camps; those who obviously enjoy a wide range of interests, and those who don't appear to do anything very much – although that may well be their choice.

There is a risk that retirement may be seen as a competition with others, rather than an opportunity for personal exploration. Whether you like the idea or not, how you manage your retirement affects not only you, but those around you, both the immediate and more distant family members. It also rubs off on friends and neighbours, as well as former work colleagues. Everyone who retires is 'watched' to see how well they are coping, and there is a questionable tendency to assume that those who are energetic and gregarious must be having a better time than the people who appreciate quieter pursuits.

Other people's interest in retirement is indicative of society's uncertain and ambivalent attitudes towards older people generally. No one is quite sure how retired people are supposed to behave.

American reactions are characteristically positive, if not downright aggressive. In the sun-belt states of California, Florida and New Mexico, there are seniors wearing T-shirts with the slogan 'Modern Grandma: I don't do cookies' while car stickers read 'We're spending our kids' inheritance'. Slogans are often irreverent pointers to the truth, if not the whole truth, and if this is the case, their message is clear. The third age is here to stay. Enjoy it . . . but do it *your* way.

About Age Concern

An Active Retirement is one of a wide range of publications produced by Age Concern England – National Council on Ageing. In addition, Age Concern is actively engaged in training, information provision, research and campaigning for retired people and those who work with them. It is a registered charity dependent on public support for the continuation of its work.

Age Concern England links closely with Age Concern centres in Scotland, Wales and Northern Ireland to form a network of over 1,400 independent local UK groups. These groups, with the invaluable help of an estimated 250,000 volunteers, aim to improve the quality of life for older people and develop services appropriate to local needs and resources. These include advice and information, day care, visiting services, transport schemes, clubs, and specialist facilities for physically and mentally frail older people.

Age Concern England
1268 London Road
London SW16 4ER
Tel: 081–679 8000

Age Concern Scotland
54A Fountainbridge
Edinburgh EH3 9PT
Tel: 031–228 5656

Age Concern Wales
4th Floor
1 Cathedral Road
Cardiff CF1 9SD
Tel: 0222 371566

Age Concern Northern Ireland
3 Lower Crescent
Belfast BT7 1NR
Tel: 0232 245729

Publications from ◆A◆C◆E Books

A wide range of titles is published by Age Concern England under the ACE Books imprint.

MONEY MATTERS

Your Rights
Sally West

A Highly acclaimed annual guide to the State Benefits available to older people. Contains current information on Income Support, Housing Benefit and retirement pensions, among other matters, and provides advice on how to claim them.

Further information on application

Your Taxes and Savings
Jennie Hawthorne and Sally West

Explains how the tax system affects people over retirement age, including how to avoid paying more tax than is necessary. The information about savings covers the wide range of investment opportunities now available.

Further information on application

Using Your Home as Capital
Cecil Hinton and David Bookbinder

This best-selling book for home-owners, which is updated annually, gives a detailed explanation of how to capitalise on the value of your home and obtain a regular additional income.

£4.50   0-86242-117-9

Earning Money in Retirement
Kenneth Lysons

Many people, for a variety of reasons, wish to continue in some form of paid employment beyond the normal retirement age. This helpful guide explores the practical implications of such a choice and highlights some of the opportunities available.

£5.95   0-86242-103-9

HOUSING

Housing Options for Older People
David Bookbinder
A review of housing options is part of growing older. All the possibilities and their practical implications are carefully considered in this comprehensive guide.
£4.95   0-86242-108-X

An Owner's Guide: Your Home in Retirement
Foreword by Christopher Chope OBE MP
This definitive guide considers all aspects of home maintenance of concern to retired people and those preparing for retirement, providing advice on heating, insulation and adaptations.
Co-published with the NHTPC.
£2.50   0-86242-095-4

GENERAL

Living, Loving and Ageing: Sexual and personal relationships in later life
Wendy Greengross and Sally Greengross
Sexuality is often regarded as the preserve of the younger generation. At last, here is a book for older people and those who work with them, which tackles the issues in a straightforward fashion, avoiding preconceptions and bias.
£4.95   0-86242-070-9

Looking Good, Feeling Good: Fashion and beauty in mid-life and beyond
Nancy Tuft
Positive, upbeat and awash with useful advice and ideas, this book encourages the over-50s to take pride in their appearance and challenges the popular view that interest in fashion and beauty passes with the years.
£7.95   0-86242-102-0

Life in the Sun: A guide to long-stay holidays and living abroad in retirement
Nancy Tuft

Every year millions of older people consider either taking long-stay holidays or moving abroad on a more permanent basis. This essential guide examines the pitfalls associated with such a move and tackles topics varying from pets to packing.

£6.95   0-86242-085-7

Gardening in Retirement
Isobel Pays

Whether a reader is new to gardening, or wishing to adapt an existing garden for more efficient maintenance, this book offers practical guidance. Illustrated in full colour.

£1.95   0-86242-039-3

HEALTH AND CARE

The Magic of Movement
Laura Mitchell

Full of encouragement, this book is for those who are finding everyday activities more difficult. Includes gentle exercises to tone up the muscles, and ideas to make you more independent and help you to avoid boredom.

£3.95   0-86242-076-8

To order books, send a cheque or money order to the address below. Postage and packing is free. Credit card orders may be made on 081-679 8000.

ACE Books
Age Concern England
PO Box 9
London SW16 4EX

Information factsheets

Age Concern England produces factsheets on a variety of subjects, and among these the following titles may be of interest to readers of this book:

Factsheet 4 *Holidays for Older People*

Factsheet 12 *Raising Income or Capital from Your Home*

Factsheet 15 *Income Tax and Older People*

Factsheet 19 *Your State Pension and Carrying on Working*

Factsheet 26 *Travel Information for Older People*

Factsheet 30 *Leisure Education*

To order factsheets
Single copies are free on receipt of a 9″ by 6″ sae. If you require a selection of factsheets or multiple copies totalling more than ten, charges will be given on request.

A complete set of factsheets is available in a ring binder at the current cost of £32, which includes the first year's subscription. The current cost for an annual subscription for subsequent years is £12. There are different rates of subscription for people living abroad.

Factsheets are revised and updated throughout the year and membership of the subscription service will ensure that your information is always current.

For further information, or to order factsheets, write to:

Information and Policy Department
Age Concern England
1268 London Road
London SW16 4ER

About the sponsor

In preparing for retirement, many people make plans to take up new hobbies or set out to explore new parts of the globe. Yet the best laid plans can go awry if personal mobility becomes restricted, perhaps through back or hip problems or arthritis.

During retirement it is important to retain a familiar way of life, and the ability to move freely around the house and continue to be independent is essential. Simple changes in the home may be all that is needed to achieve this.

The effort of everyday tasks can be virtually eliminated by labour-saving devices, so that hobbies and leisure activities can be enjoyed to the full. A dishwasher, microwave oven, sit-on lawnmower or a stairlift can help conserve personal energy for more pleasurable pursuits, such as gardening, swimming, or other recreational activities.

Stannah Stairlifts, the world's leading domestic stairlift manufacturer, believes that one of the vital ingredients to enjoying a happy retirement is the need to remain active and maintain independence. Many of us have witnessed friends or relatives who, though fiercely independent in many respects, experience difficulties getting around their home and managing household tasks on their own.

A survey recently carried out on behalf of Stannah revealed that over a million people living in Great Britain find climbing the stairs a problem. The findings showed that on average people go up and down the stairs 13 times a day, using up to 10–15 calories a minute, which is roughly the same as running up a hill or cross-country skiing!

Stannah is renowned for taking the strain out of everyday life, preserving your energies for the other activities you look forward to. The Company has designed a range of stylish stairlifts – both indoor and outdoor – to help you continue enjoying an active retirement by gaining easy access in and around the home.

The Stannah Stairlift range comprises four different models which can follow nearly every type of stairway, coping with intermediate landings, bends, travelling along corridors, even all the way up in a spiral. New colour schemes including two body colours and eight colours for the trim have been chosen after careful analysis of trends in fabric colours and textures for interior decoration worldwide.

Whether your stairs are straight or complex, a Stannah Stairlift allows you to glide up and down your stairs safely, without effort. You do not need to consider moving home to a flat or bungalow. Installation is carried out by skilled fitters and the stairlift can be in place within a few hours without so much as a speck of dust left on the carpet.

Safety in the home is seldom more important than when dealing with mobility problems and you can rest assured about the quality of Stannah Stairlifts. This is evidenced by the Company being awarded certification to British Standard 5750 on quality, as well as the products being certified to British Standard 5776. Stannah prides itself on its excellent customer care programme and with a nationwide network of local branches, can provide a fast, reliable and efficient service 365 days a year.

Since it was established in 1835 by Joseph Stannah, the Company has been a leading British lift manufacturer. Stannah's products encompass the complete spectrum of passenger, industrial and special purpose lifts. Stannah Stairlifts is the world's largest manufacturer of stairlifts, with installations in over 30 countries.

The Company has gained the reputation of a world class lift manufacturer by offering the highest standards in product development, coupled with unbeatable personal service.

If you would like further details on the range of Stannah Stairlifts available, simply pick up the phone, dial 0800 378 386 free of charge and ask for extension 707. Let us show you how you can improve the quality of your leisure time and enjoy an active retirement for years to come!

Index